SCHOOLS
and DATA

SCHOOLS
and DATA

THE EDUCATOR'S GUIDE
FOR USING DATA TO IMPROVE
DECISION MAKING

THEODORE B. CREIGHTON

CORWIN PRESS, INC.
A Sage Publications Company
Thousand Oaks, California

For information:

Corwin Press, Inc.
A Sage Publications Company
2455 Teller Road
Thousand Oaks, California 91320
E-mail: order@corwinpress.com

Sage Publications Ltd.
6 Bonhill Street
London EC2A 4PU
United Kingdom

Sage Publications India Pvt. Ltd.
M-32 Market
Greater Kailash I
New Delhi 110 048 India

Printed in the United States of America

Library of Congress Cataloging-in-Publication Data

Creighton, Theodore B.
    Schools and data: The educator's guide for using data to improve decision making / by Theodore B. Creighton.
        p.   cm.
    Includes bibliographical references and index.
    ISBN 0-7619-7716-3 (cloth: alk. paper)
    ISBN 0-7619-7717-1 (pbk.: alk. paper)
    1. School management and organization—Statistical methods.
    2. Decision making—Statistical methods.   I. Title.
    LB2805 .C737   2000
    371.2′002′1—dc21   00-008771

This book is printed on acid-free paper.

01   02   03   04   05   06   07   7   6   5   4   3   2

Corwin Editorial Assistant:	Kylee Liegl
Production Editor:	Nevair Kabakian
Editorial Assistant:	Candice Crosetti
Typesetter/Designer:	Lynn Miyata
Cover Designer:	Tracy E. Miller

Contents

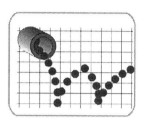

List of Figures and Tables

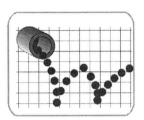

Preface

Few would deny that the main responsibility for the decision-making process in our schools has been assumed by building and central office administrators and that education leaders are now asking (and expecting) classroom teachers to participate in this decision making as well. For too long, many school leaders have made decisions about instructional leadership with "intuition" and "shooting from the hip." All too often, school leaders do not include data collection and data analysis in the decision-making process.

We are realizing that meaningful information can be gained only from a proper analysis of data and that good decisions are based on this thoughtful process of inquiry and analysis. School districts across the nation collect and maintain many forms of educational data (e.g., attendance rates, standardized and criterion-referenced test scores); however, most schools use the collection of these data to satisfy administrative requirements rather than to assess and evaluate school improvement. Educators rarely examine these data to assess in a systematic way the quality of teaching and learning at their school. This book addresses the dire need for an approach to statistical analysis that is related to educational leadership decision-making applications.

This need will only become greater as society and our state departments of education ask for more accountability from our school leaders. The good news is that the advances in technology make the collection of school data almost automatic. Principals and teachers must possess an understanding of data analysis and ways to use this analysis to improve teaching and learning in the classroom.

Fewer things are more feared than the thought of "statistical analysis." To most educators, statistics means endless calculations and memorization of formulas. Statistics is seen by most as a formal domain of advanced mathematics and represented by a course or two taught by professors desiring to make a student's life as painful as possible. Courses in statistical methods are usually taught with formal proofs of mathematical theorems and the derivation of statistical formulas as a main focus.

Is this anxiety and fear due to the fact that statistical analysis requires a level of mathematical knowledge beyond the capabilities of principals and teachers? If someone has passed a high school course in elementary algebra, he or she has acquired all the knowledge and skills required for an understanding of statistical analysis (Runyan, Haber, & Coleman, 1994). Students report that their fear is mostly related to the fact that statistics has no relevance to solving the many issues in our day-to-day living (Creighton, 1999).

The educator's fear of statistics probably relates to a variety of factors, but principal and teacher preparation programs must accept that the presentation of statistics in education probably lacks four important components. First, it does not emphasize the relevance of statistics to the day-to-day lives of principals and teachers. Second, it does not fully integrate current technology into the teaching and learning of statistics. Third, few (if any) statistics courses are designed for students enrolled in teacher education or education leadership programs. Fourth, and finally, many statistics courses taught in colleges of education devote a major part of their time to inferential statistics as a tool in conducting research projects and dissertations. Far less time is spent on statistical strategies that might help the principal or teacher improve their skills in problem analysis, program and student evaluation, data-based decision making, and report preparation (McNamara, 1996).

Schools and Data: The Educator's Guide for Using Data to Improve Decision Making addresses the above mentioned four issues. A brief description of each follows.

Relevance of Statistics to the Lives of Principals and Teachers

Traditional courses in statistics result in the frequent student response: "When will I ever use this stuff?" This book gives examples, data sets, and problems centered on a wide range of real-world data distributions used by principals and teachers in their work. In addition, actual class projects completed by principals and teachers in the field are presented in each chapter.

Integration of Recent Technology Into the Teaching and Learning of Statistics

The teaching of applied educational statistics needs to move away from the traditional conception of statistics as mathematical theory and closer to administrator and teacher preparation programs (McNamara, 1996). The advance of technology and the large selection of user-friendly computer software assist us as we make this move toward a more practical and relevant presentation of statistics for educators. Though several good statistical packages exist, two leading statistical packages are used throughout this book: (a) GB-STAT and (b) Statistical Package for the Social Sciences (SPSS). Both are easy-to-use, menu-driven statistical programs applicable for analyzing such data as student standardized test scores, attendance and dropout rates, and college entrance requirements.

Though we agree with the importance of educators' learning to calculate statistics, the early and regular use of GB-STAT and/or SPSS allows the student and practitioner to spend less time on complex mathematical calculations and more time on statistical selection and interpretation. Step-by-step procedures are presented in each chapter of this book, accompanied by actual applications to educators' problems in the field.

Statistical Analysis Designed for Educators

This book centers on a master's-level statistics course titled "Applied Educational Statistics for Principal and Teacher Preparation," taught in the

Department of Education Leadership at Idaho State University. The students, whose projects are included in each chapter, are practicing teachers working on a master's degree in education leadership and preparing for the principalship. The data are collected from real classrooms, focusing on student instruction and assessment, attendance and dropout rates, college entrance tests, and instructional program evaluations.

Descriptive and Inferential Statistics

Though inferential statistics are more likely to be used in research studies and dissertations, descriptive statistics are more likely to be used in the schools. Descriptive statistics (percentile ranks, means, median, modes, range, standard deviation) help us *describe* those studied, and inferential statistics use sample data to *estimate* parameters and test hypotheses. In most cases, the educator encounters data in the schools that are related to populations rather than samples. In other words, data are collected from entire classes or grade levels, entire building populations, and entire district populations. Principals and teachers are not interested in generalizing their school data findings to other schools or estimating parameters and test hypotheses. Their immediate interest is in data from their school for the current academic year (McNamara, 1996). Though much of this book's emphasis will be on descriptive data analysis, I include many examples of how the educator can use inferential statistical analysis. I attempt to shift the use of inferential analysis from the traditional research and dissertation model to one of relevance and applicability to teachers and administrators.

Acknowledgments

Someone once stated that an author is essentially the pen through which significant others write. In this case, the significant others are the many education leaders participating in the Master's and Doctoral Program in Education Leadership at Idaho State University. Though I highlight only a few in this book, I am grateful to all of the master's and doctoral students at the university who helped me turn this thing called "statistics" into a meaningful and comprehensible experience for our teachers and administrators.

I am especially grateful to the Idaho State University doctoral cohort who kindly and willingly used this book as a supplemental resource during their applied educational statistics course taken in Spring 2000. Their comments and constructive suggestions were appreciated and contributed greatly to the final copy currently in your hands.

The creation of tables and figures is a critical component of a book such as this. Christopher Williams, a current doctoral student in educational leadership, and Cristan Miles, a teacher education major, deserve my thanks and appreciation for a job well done.

The greatest editor and proofreader is from my household—my wife Linda. The number of hours spent reading copy and editing my silly mistakes are beyond counting.

Corwin Press would like to acknowledge the following reviewers:

Hank Becker
University of California, Irvine
Irvine, CA

Phillip Leahy
University of New York
New York, NY

Scott McLeod
University of Cincinnati
Cincinatti, OH

Marie Miller-Whitehead
The Miller Group
Alexandria, VA

Paul G. Preuss
The Herkeimer BOCES
Herkeimer, NY

Jacob Stampen
University of Wisconsin - Madison
Madison, WI

Karen L. Tichy
Catholic Education Office, Archdiocese of St. Louis
St. Louis, MO

About the Author

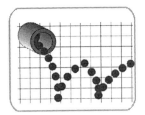

Theodore B. Creighton is currently Associate Professor at the Center for Research and Doctoral Studies in Educational Leadership at Sam Houston State University, where he teaches research and instructional leadership at both the master's and doctoral levels. He previously served as Coordinator of Principal Preparation Program in the Department of Education Leadership at Idaho State University (ISU), where he taught courses in the principalship, change strategies, school personnel, and applied educational statistics for principals and teachers. He also serves as a member of the Intermountain Center for Education Effectiveness, a K-16 service organization for schools in the Intermountain area. In addition, he is the Senior Editor of the *Journal of the Intermountain Center.* Prior to joining the faculty at ISU, he served on the faculty at the University of Wyoming as a Professor in Teacher Education. His background includes teaching at all grade levels in Washington, D.C.; Cleveland, Ohio; and Los Angeles, California. His administrative experience includes serving as principal and superintendent in both Fresno and Kern Counties, California. He holds a B.S. in teacher education from Indiana University of Pennsylvania, master's degrees in educational administration from Kent State University and California State University Long Beach, and a doctorate from the Fresno State University/University of California Joint Doctoral Program. Though active in many professional organizations, he devotes much of his time working with the National Council of Professors of Educational Administration (NCPEA), where he sits on the Executive Board. He recently chaired the 1999 NCPEA National Conference in Jackson Hole, Wyoming. His research includes examining the forces of the school principalship, and he is widely published in the area of schools with alternative forms of school leadership. Specifically, he has completed extensive research of schools without principals.

1 The Role of Statistics in the Lives of Teachers and Principals

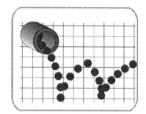

During my many years as a classroom teacher and then as a principal and district superintendent of schools, I especially questioned the enormous amount of time we spent in collecting numbers. Thirty to 40 minutes each morning were spent in collecting and reporting attendance. The annual state-mandated testing procedure began in early October and seemed to exist in one form or another for the entire year. But we collected our scores, sent them to the office, and never saw them again.

School districts across the nation collect and maintain many forms of educational data. Standardized test scores, average daily attendance figures, and transcript data are required by states for funding purposes. However, most schools use the collection of these data to satisfy administrative requirements rather than to assess and evaluate school improvement. Standardized test scores are generally reviewed only briefly before the local newspaper calls. Average daily attendance is reported to state education agencies, then filed away someplace. Educators rarely examine these data to assess in a systematic way the quality of teaching and learning at their school (MPR Associates, 1998).

What Is This Thing Called Statistics?

First of all, statistics is not advanced mathematics. The majority of statistical analyses useful to the principal and teacher can be completed with a basic understanding of mathematics and involve conceptual understanding more than complex calculations. Statistics is a set of tools designed to help *describe* the sample or population from which the data were gathered and to *explain* the possible relationship between variables.

> A school principal wonders if the mathematics instruction in his school is being delivered in a manner that does not favor either boys or girls. In other words, is mathematics being presented in an equitable manner at his school? A simple statistical procedure called the *Pearson correlation* can help identify a relationship between math scores and gender (this procedure, along with the GB-STAT and SPSS steps, will be presented in detail in Chapter 10). If the results of the analysis indicate that there is a pattern of boys' receiving higher scores in mathematics on standardized tests, the principal may want to look more closely at classroom instruction to determine if perhaps instructional strategies can be altered to address the equity issue.

> A seventh-grade language arts teacher is interested to know if there is a relationship between students' performance on the district writing assessment and their socioeconomic level. In other words, do students who come from lower socioeconomic backgrounds *really* perform lower, as we are led to believe? Or are other variables responsible for the variance in writing performance? Again, a simple correlation analysis will help *describe* the students' performance and help *explain* the relationship between the issues of performance and socioeconomic level.

Data analysis does not have to involve complex statistics. Data analysis in schools involves (a) collecting data and (b) using available data for the purpose of improving teaching and learning. Interestingly enough, principals and teachers have it pretty easy—in most cases, the collection of data has already been done. Schools regularly collect attendance data, transcript records, discipline referrals, quarterly or semester grades, norm and criterion reference test scores, and a variety of other useful data. Generally, we are interested not so much in complex statistical formulas and tests as in simple counts, averages, percentages, and rates. We will cover more of this later.

What Are GB-STAT and SPSS?

The Statistical Package for the Social Sciences (SPSS) and GB-STAT are common computer software programs designed to allow people in the social sciences to analyze their data. They can tabulate the numbers of male and female students in a school, calculate average grades of the students, compare test scores by gender, determine if there is a statistically significant difference between achievement of athletes and nonathletes, compare computer-assisted instruction with other methods of delivery, and so on. GB-STAT and SPSS display frequency distributions and cross-tabulations and calculate descriptive statistics (mean, mode, median, range, interquartile range, standard deviation) in addition to inferential statistics (chi-square, Pearson correlation coefficients, regression, etc.).

This book uses GB-STAT and SPSS for Windows throughout for examples and illustrations. Becoming familiar with GB-STAT and/or SPSS will not be a disadvantage to individuals ending up in a school using other computer software programs (e.g., Minitab, SAS). Good complete versions of GB-STAT and SPSS are reasonably priced, with even lower prices on the horizon.

The Rationale for Using Data to Improve Decision Making in Our Schools

Much recent research indicates why school leaders must become familiar with and use existing school data to make sound educational decisions about teaching and learning (Fitch & Malcom, 1998; McNamara, 1996). Most recently, the National Science Foundation and the National Center for Educational Statistics developed an information management and data-warehousing system that provides school leaders with easy-to-use access to all of their data (http://nces.ed.gov/). The system focuses on how best to use these technologies for effective school leadership and improved decision making. James McNamara (1996), from Texas A & M University, has written extensively on teaching statistics in principal preparation programs. His research helps answer the question "What aspects of statistical methods should be emphasized in a basic statistics course that is designed explicitly to help school principals improve their skills in problem analysis, program evaluation, data-based decision making, and report preparation?"

A master's-level statistics course is a core course requirement in the education leadership and teacher education programs at Idaho State University. This course has traditionally been presented as mathematical theory in a computational manner. Recently, the departments of education administration and teacher education refocused the instructional delivery to help principals and teachers improve their skills in problem analysis, instructional program evaluation, report preparation, and data-driven decision making. A purpose of the course is to provide principals and teachers the skills and experience necessary to use data analysis for school improvement, with special attention given to increasing student achievement. Students bring real-life data sets from their classrooms and spend the semester analyzing the data as we move through the standard statistical procedures such as frequency distributions, means, standard deviations, Pearson correlations, chi-squares, and linear regression. This instructional strategy emphasizes the relevance of statistics to the day-to-day lives of principals and teachers.

So, What's the Problem?

Holcomb's very successful book *Getting Excited About Data* (1999) discussed why data are little used in our schools and why it is so difficult to generate passion to get educators engaged:

> My observations are that more than half of our teachers have graduate degrees and have taken at least one course in tests and measurements or statistics. I have four graduate degrees myself and can recall no class discussion of what to do with assessment information in planning how to help students do better. I have come to the conclusions that such courses are taught by researchers as though they are preparing researchers.
>
> As a result, the emphasis is on esoteric experimental design—which can't be replicated in a normal school setting. (p. 22)

Holcomb continued by quoting Gerald Bracey (1997), internationally recognized as one of the country's respected experts in the understanding of education statistics:

Many of the university professors who create and use statistics are more comfortable using them than they are teaching other human beings what they mean. And in all too many instances, statistics are taught in a theoretically rarefied atmosphere replete with hard-to-understand formulas and too few examples to the daily life of education practitioners. (p. 22)

I agree with Holcomb and also state that the uses of data suggested in this book are not likely to meet the academic standards required in dissertations. The book's purpose is to illustrate how statistical analysis can be applied to everyday situations found in our schools. The book can be used as a refresher course for all educators who probably had some courses in applied statistics but have never found a way to use what they were taught.

The Use of Statistics in the
Classroom and Principal's Office:
A Case Study

Karla, who taught grades 3 and 4 mathematics at a small rural K-8 school district in southeastern Idaho, was interested in finding out if a mathematics series adopted by the district 5 years earlier was effective for all levels of students. Karla's hypothesis was:

The district math program is effective with middle- and low-ability students but doesn't address the needs of students with above-average math ability.

Her hypothesis was based upon the belief that the district math program overemphasized computation and repetition but lacked the components of in-depth investigations and problem-solving experiences. To help answer the research hypothesis, she collected 4 years of Iowa Test of Basis Skills (ITBS) percentile rank scores on her students. She created the following procedures:

Step 1. Ranking the students into categories of high, medium, and low. Karla based her grouping on the percentile rank scores from the first-year baseline data and categorized students scoring at or above the 60th percentile as the high group, students scoring at or above the 40th and below the 60th percentile as the medium group, and students scoring below the 40th percentile as the low group.

Step 2. Creating a data file. Using SPSS Windows, Karla entered the students' ITBS percentile ranks into a spreadsheet.

Step 3. Analyze the data. With a few simple mouse clicks on her computer, she discovered that:

a. All (100%) of her students who were rated "below average" increased their scores over the 4-year period.

b. An unusually high number (75%) of her students who were rated "above average" revealed a decline in their scores over the same 4-year period.

After running a few more statistical tests with her student data, Karla presented her findings to her principal and superintendent. She was invited to share her data analysis with the board of education. Though realizing that her analysis did not necessarily prove anything, she felt that the discovered pattern indicated a need for reevaluating the math program and especially her teaching methods in the classroom. Karla's conclusion to the superintendent and board was that the district math program seemed to be challenging the lower level of students by reinforcing basic skills but that the higher level of students (having already achieved the fundamentals) needed additional instruction to apply, inquire, and experiment with the numbers and mathematical concepts they already knew.

The end of this story was the implementation by Karla and her colleagues of an enrichment math program that encouraged the higher-level students to think mathematically, apply this thinking to complex and multidimensional math problems, and communicate this thinking clearly.

Application Activities

1. Take an informal tour of your building office and the central office in your school district. Make a list of all the different kinds of data your district collects (e.g., standardized and performance-based test scores and atten-

dance, dropout, and graduation rates). Make special note of the data that seem to go nowhere. In other words, how much of what your district collects is done to satisfy state and federal requirements and is then merely filed away someplace?

2. Review this statement from the preface: "The educator's fear of statistics probably relates to a variety of factors, but principal and teacher preparation programs must accept that the presentation of statistics in education probably lacks important components." What advice would you offer to those of us who are responsible for teacher and administrator preparation programs at the university level? How might we better address data analysis in our preparation programs? Do you feel that this "fear of data and statistics" really exists, and can the fear be reduced or eliminated in our later years?

2 Getting Started

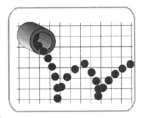

Assuming that you are still a bit nervous about the "S" word, and perhaps still unconvinced that teachers and principals can use statistics easily to help with the day-to-day decisions we need to make, let's look at a simple example of how statistics can be used to help increase student achievement. We start with a statistic all of us are comfortable with already—percentages. Table 2.1 describes a 10th-grade English class involved in a study.

There are a total of 122 students in 10th grade at Westside High School, with 10 more males than females (54% – 46% = 8%; 8% of 122 = 9.76 or 10). We use percentages every day to describe the average daily attendance, students receiving "free and reduced lunch," number of teachers with advanced degrees, and so on. Let's use this same statistic and add some other statistical information to further describe our group (Table 2.2).

Remember, percentile ranks give us a picture of where students are scoring when compared to national averages. We see that 11 females scored in the 25th percentile, with 6 males scoring in the 25th percentile. We now have a clearer picture of our 10th graders and their achievement level in mathematics. A greater number of our female students are scoring in the 25th and 50th percentiles. In addition, more of our male students are scoring at a higher level (e.g., 75th and 99th percentiles). Does this *prove* that boys are smarter than girls in mathematics? Does this *prove* that girls are less interested in mathematics? Certainly not! But our data show a pattern that warrants a further look at what is happening in our 10th-grade math curriculum. Actually, we should look at several previous grades to determine if the same pattern exists over time. Our classroom instruction and

TABLE 2.1 Gender of Westside High School 10th Graders

Sex	No.	%
Females	56	46
Males	66	54

TABLE 2.2 Westside High School 10th Graders' ITBS Math Percentile Ranks by Gender ($N = 122$)

	Females	Males
25th percentile	11	6
50th percentile	30	20
75th percentile	10	30
99th percentile	5	10

activities may show favoritism toward the male students. Our entire mathematics faculty may be male and may demonstrate an unknowing and unconscious instructional delivery weighted toward the male students. Or none of the above may be the case, and some entirely different variables may be at work (e.g., more females may be limited English speaking). However, the pattern in test scores forces us to take a close look at our curriculum, teaching, and assessment. This leads us to *data-driven decision making*. Before we look specifically at data-driven decision making, let's look at one more example of analyzing some of the data that exist in our schools.

As administrators, we are all familiar with collecting average daily attendance (ADA) figures. These numbers provide the formula used to receive our funding from the state and federal governments. In most cases, once we report the attendance to our county office or state department, we put the data away in a file someplace. Rarely do we use these data to make decisions about curriculum and instruction. Let's return to Westside High School and look at their average daily attendance rates for 1996, 1997, and 1998. The Westside attendance data are displayed in Table 2.3.

TABLE 2.3 Average Daily Attendance at Westside High School

Year	% Attending
1996	94
1997	92
1998	94

TABLE 2.4 Westside High School Attendance on a Daily Basis

Day	% Attending
Monday	95
Tuesday	95
Wednesday	97
Thursday	91
Friday	89

At first glance, things look impressive. On average, over a 3-year peri-od, 93% of our students are in school every day. We reason that 93% is kind of like an "A" and is pretty good. So we report the figures to the appropriate agencies and move on with life. But let's take a closer look. If 93% of our students are in attendance on average, we must conclude that 7% of our students are absent on average. So in fact, on average, our high school students miss nearly 2 weeks of school per year. We calculate this by taking 7% of the 180 school days ($180 \times .07 = 12.60$). Wow! Now that's a different story. Do we not agree that missing 13 days of school (on average) has curriculum and instruction ramifications? Are there ways of adjusting our curriculum, scheduling, and delivery of instruction that might help us reduce the number of absences at Westside High School? Let's *disaggregate* or break our data down a bit further. Table 2.4 breaks down our attendance rate on a daily basis.

Now we see a different picture! With no great surprise, we notice an up-and-down attendance pattern during the week. But when looking at our curriculum, scheduling, and extracurricular activities, we notice that the highest attendance rate is on Wednesday—the day we hold our football rally! In addition, we notice our lowest attendance rate is on Friday—the day most of our testing and assessment takes place! Perhaps the principal should consider changing the football rally to Friday and encourage teachers to do more of their testing on other days.

The above examples illustrate how easy it is to use existing data to help us with the day-to-day operation of our school. Hopefully, you feel a bit more at ease with the approach this book takes in demonstrating to principals and teachers the use of data analysis and how we link data analysis to what we spend our lives with—curriculum, instruction, assessment, and student achievement.

What Is Data-Driven Decision Making?

Collecting data without purpose is meaningless. All too often, school leaders fail to formulate decisions based on data. The effective use of data must play a major role in the development of school improvement plans (Fitch & Malcom, 1998). Too many of our school leaders make decisions based on "informed intuition." Meaningful information can be gained only from a proper analysis of data.

Using the many different kinds of data collected at our school site to help with decision making legitimizes the goals and strategies we create for change and improvement. It helps us identify groups of students who are improving and groups of students who are not—and helps to identify the reasons. Thus the principal can serve as instructional leader. Data-driven decision making and instructional leadership must go hand in hand.

Introduction to SPSS and GB-STAT

Earlier in the chapter, we discovered that a simple descriptive statistic such as percentages can help us answer many questions about our school and students. Does statistical analysis get any harder than this? Yes, perhaps! However, with the help of advanced statistical software packages such as SPSS and GB-STAT, there is no longer a need to understand advanced mathematical formulas—or use them, for that matter. Most statistical analysis is as easy as pointing and clicking. Let's roll up our sleeves and take a look at both of these programs.

Though GB-STAT and SPSS run on both Macintosh and Windows, we will refer to the Windows platform for SPSS and the Mac platform for GB-STAT throughout to give you a choice of programs and platforms. The two programs and platforms are so similar that no one should have any difficulty moving from one to the other. Let's begin with a brief overview of using GB-STAT for Macintosh.

Getting Started With GB-STAT for Macintosh

The purpose of this example is to demonstrate how quickly and easily you may begin to analyze data with GB-STAT for Macintosh. Step-by-step instruction is provided to show how a variable-by-case data matrix may be opened from the disk and manipulated. In addition, the concept of importing data files will be presented.

Data Entry Options

From the main menu bar, choose the leftmost option, called **File.** A drop-down menu will give you a variety of data entry options. Among the choices, GB-STAT provides you with the options of creating a new database from the keyboard (**New**), opening an already created data file (**Open**), or importing a data file from another program (**Import**). We often create our files with spreadsheet programs such as Excel or Quattro Pro: Importing to GB-STAT is very easy.

Opening a GB-STAT Formatted Data File

To open a GB-STAT data file from the main menu bar, choose **File** and then **Open.** This opens the Open Data File box. You can then select a file name from the list that appears on the screen.

Importing a Spreadsheet File

It is very easy to bring in data produced from spreadsheets such as Excel. GB-STAT will import data files in which the values have been separated by delimiters (e.g., commas, spaces, or tabs). When in Excel with your data file, select **Save As** and select a file type of **Text.** This will create a tab-delimited file of your Excel spreadsheet. If your Excel file contains text data (words), be sure to end the variable name with a "$" so that GB-STAT will properly import the data. Now, when in GB-STAT, select **Import** and then **Text File**; accept the default suggestions in the Import dialog box, and select the Excel text file you just saved. GB-STAT will read the Excel file and place the data in a new GB-STAT data grid. In addition to this process, you can always use the standard **Copy** and **Paste** functions to copy data from Excel (for example) and paste data into a highlighted area in the GB-STAT data matrix.

Getting Started With SPSS for Windows

Using SPSS for Windows is very similar to the procedures presented above for GB-STAT. After entering the Windows environment, use the mouse to select (point and click once) the SPSS for Windows icon. When you open SPSS, a slightly different screen appears. The following menu will appear on your monitor:

▶ Run the Tutorial

▶ Type in Data

▶ Run an Existing Query

▶ Create New Query Using Database Capture Wizard

▶ Open an Existing File

To begin with, you may wish to select **Run the Tutorial** and click on **Open.** Several options appear that will assist you in touring the SPSS program. Enjoy!

Creating an SPSS Data File

Going back to the menu mentioned above, select **Type in Data,** and an empty spreadsheet will appear. You are now ready to input data from your classroom, office, or school.

Labeling Variables

Variables are named in the columns across the top of the spreadsheet. To give each a name (e.g., Itbsmath, Itbsread, or Itbsscie), click twice on the cell labeled *VAR.* A dialog box will appear that allows you to name your column (limit of eight characters). Click **OK,** and you return to your data spreadsheet. Continue double-clicking on the separate columns until all your variables are named.

Entering Your Data

The spreadsheet rows are in numerical order and represent your individual classes, students, interview respondents, and so on. Let's suppose we want to type in the Iowa Test of Basic Skills (ITBS) math score for our first student (Row Number 1). Highlight the cell, and simply type in the score and hit RETURN or one of the arrow keys. Continue the process until all of your data have been typed into appropriate cells.

Saving Your Data File

It is important to save your work often. Select **File** from the menu at the top of your screen, select **Save As,** and a screen appears that asks you to name the file. It is important that you also select the location you desire for the file in the box titled "Save In" (e.g., hard drive, disk, or desktop). Select **OK,** and your work is saved in the location you selected. You can now add more data, rename existing variables, or begin your data analysis.

Let's Try an Example

We are going to create a GB-STAT or SPSS data file of ITBS math scores for a class of sixth graders to determine if there might be a correlation

TABLE 2.5 Westside High School Sixth Graders' ITBS Math and Reading Scores by Gender

Student	Gender	Math	Reading
1	Female	230	222
2	Male	245	230
3	Female	210	200
4	Male	235	235
5	Male	220	215

between their math and reading scores. In other words, we want to see if in fact students who have a tendency to score high in math also score high in reading (and if students who tend to score low in math also tend to score low in reading). If so, perhaps we can help demonstrate to our teachers the importance of collaborative instructional strategies across the two disciplines. If not, we might want to ask some further questions about why this is not the case. While we are collecting data, we might also want to know the gender of each student so that we can also look at the relationship between achievement and gender. To simplify the process, we will use data from only five students. The data are shown in Table 2.5.

Table 2.6 displays the results of the Data Matrix grid with GB-STAT for Macintosh, and Table 2.7 displays the same data using the SPSS for Windows platform. You will notice an almost identical look.

An important note: when typing in text data (e.g., student's name or gender), GB-STAT requires that the variable name be followed by a $; SPSS requires that you change the variable type setting from numeric to string (numbers to a word).

Conclusion

You will hear me say several times throughout this book that we must be careful not to move too quickly into the use of computer software to ana-

TABLE 2.6 GB-STAT Matrix Grid for Sixth Graders' ITBS Math and
              Reading Scores by Gender

Student	Name$	Gender$	Math	Reading
1	Karen	Female	230	222
2	Tom	Male	245	230
3	Susan	Female	210	235
4	Paul	Male	235	235
5	Richard	Male	220	215

TABLE 2.7 SPSS Matrix Grid for Sixth Graders' ITBS Math and Reading
              Scores by Gender

Student	Name	Gender	Math	Reading
1	Karen	Female	230	222
2	Tom	Male	245	230
3	Susan	Female	210	200
4	Paul	Male	235	235
5	Richard	Male	220	215

lyze our data. Having said this, let me say I also agree that we are increasingly provided with excellent computer software that makes calculations for us very quickly. My particular excitement with the new computer software is that it allows us to spend less time with calculations and formulas and more time with analysis and interpretation. We can now concern ourselves with the actual problems at hand and looking for practical solutions to them. In Chapter 3, we will begin to work with some real-life school data. Press on!

Application Activities

1. Using either GB-STAT or SPSS, open a new data file. Create a sample file by inputting the following information. Label the students' names

(Variable 1) as *Students,* and label the test scores as *Scores.* Because Variable 1 is "words," you must either use the "$" with GB-STAT or change the option for variable to **String** in SPSS. In SPSS, after double-clicking on the variable column, a screen appears asking you to define the variable. Remember, to change from numeric to string, select **Type,** and you will be able to change the setting from numeric to string. Obviously, Variable 2 is numeric, so you will need to change the setting back to numeric. Practice saving the file to your desktop.

2. From an existing Excel spreadsheet file (or creating a small sample), use your **Copy** function to copy a column or two of data. Close the Excel file, and open GB-STAT or SPSS. Select a cell and **Paste** the data in the new file. SPSS allows you to select one cell where your data will begin. GB-STAT, on the other hand, requires you to highlight the entire numbers of cells your new data will occupy. Again, practice saving your new file to the desktop.

3 Collecting and Organizing Data

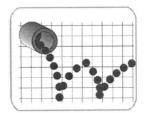

Westside High School is a small rural district in central California with an enrollment of 135 students in grades 9 through 12. The administration for several years has been trying to encourage teachers to consider collaborative instructional strategies across disciplines and grade levels. The staff at Westside High School, like many others, feels pretty strongly that "math is math," and "language is language," and never shall the two disciplines overlap. After all, students need separate instruction in each of these important subjects.

Michael Johnston, the high school principal, decides to take a look at last year's standardized test scores, along with some student demographic data such as socioeconomic status, gender, ethnicity, and participation in extracurricular activities. Maybe he can use this information to help his teachers understand the relationship between disciplines. His hunch is that there might be a relationship between math and language scores. If so, maybe this information will help the staff see the connection between instruction and some of the other information we collect.

To begin our preliminary analysis of data, we must first create a Westside High School data file in SPSS or GB-STAT. You are encouraged to create your own file from scratch (your own students) and follow along with our procedures in this chapter. It will be easy to follow me using your own students and their scores. Don't be afraid to use your own variables—you may have an interest in collecting other data.

TABLE 3.1 Gender of Westside Students

Gender	No.	%
Male	72	53
Female	63	47
Total	135	100

TABLE 3.2 Ethnicity of Westside Students

Ethnicity	No.	%
White	65	48
Hispanic	32	24
Black	14	10
Native American	24	18

Frequency Distribution

A sample distribution allows the educator to see general trends more easily than does an unordered set of scores. A frequency distribution is a listing, in order of magnitude of each score achieved (or any variable), together with the number of times that the score occurred.

We now want to take a close look at some demographic characteristics of our group of high school students. In other words, what does our group look like? Are they largely from low socioeconomic backgrounds? Are they predominantly male? Is there a high percentage on the football and basketball teams? To get at some of these questions, we must have an understanding of how to obtain and interpret *frequency distributions* with SPSS or GB-STAT.

Michael first takes a look at the gender and ethnicity of the students at Westside High School. Tables 3.1 and 3.2 show the results.

Frequency distributions help us describe the characteristics of the population we are studying. Our Westside High School students are approximately half male and half female, but they represent a variety of cultural and ethnic backgrounds. Will an understanding of these characteristics help us as we design appropriate teaching and learning strategies for Westside High School? Let's go on with our analysis and see.

Creating Frequency Distributions

With the help of SPSS and GB-STAT, creating frequency distributions is easy. Open the data file from SPSS or GB-STAT. From the menu at the top of the screen, select **Statistics,** then **Frequency Distribution.** A dialog box appears, allowing you to select the variables on which you want frequency distributions. Click the mouse on the variable you want from the left box, and by clicking on the arrow you can move the variable to the right box (a shortcut is to simply double-click the variable, which automatically moves the variable to the right). Select **OK,** and the frequencies will appear in the output window.

If you decide to look at another frequency distribution, simply return to the dialog box and repeat the procedure with the desired variables. Clicking **OK** shows the frequency in the output window in addition to the first frequency. In other words, the output window keeps track of all your frequency reports. When you close the window, SPSS asks you if you want to **Save** the information in the window. If so, simply select **Save** and give the file a name. This allows you to view your frequencies at a later time.

Cross-Tabulation

The **Frequency** command can tell us that at Westside High School there are 65 white, 32 Hispanic, 14 black, and 24 Native American students (and that there are 72 males and 63 females). But it cannot show us how many female Hispanic or male black students we have in our school. Both GB-STAT and SPSS can help us answer these questions with the help of the **Crosstabs** command. **Crosstabs** simply allows us to "cross" two variables (e.g., ethnicity and gender). The result is shown in Table 3.3.

Don't hesitate to try crossing more than two variables (e.g., ethnicity, gender, and socioeconomic status). Both GB-STAT and SPSS can handle that easily. After selecting **Crosstabs,** just move your desired variables from the list on the left part of the screen to the box on the right. As stated earlier,

TABLE 3.3 Westside Students, Ethnicity by Gender

	Gender		
Ethnicity	*Male (n)*	*Female (n)*	*Total (N)*
White	33	32	65
Hispanic	16	16	32
Black	11	3	14
Native American	12	12	24
Total	72	63	135

statistical analysis does not have to be complicated or complex. However, before we go too much further, we must take a few minutes to discuss measures of central tendency and measures of variability. This information will help us as we go forward with analyzing the various kinds of data found in schools.

Measures of Central Tendency

The most common method for summarizing and describing a set of test scores is to compute the average. In statistics, the concept of averaging is called *central tendency*. Quite simply, the goal of central tendency is to find the average or typical score that provides a reasonably accurate description of a whole class or grade level, for example.

From earlier training in grade school and junior high, we remember that finding the *mean* (first measure of central tendency) involves adding up all the scores and dividing by the total number of students in the distribution. For example, looking at our Westside High School data file, we calculate the mean math score by adding all 135 scores together, then dividing by 135. Wow! Too time consuming, you say? I agree—and too many chances for silly mistakes when adding up all those numbers.

The good news is that as we do our analyses with GB-STAT and SPSS, we always have the option to ask the computer to add that measure of central tendency to our printout. You probably remember the other two measures of central tendency: the *median* and the *mode.* The median is the score that falls exactly in the middle of the distribution (0.5 if an odd number), and the mode is the most frequently occurring score.

Let's give it a try. Using our Westside High School data, ask for a frequency distribution of math scores. Select **Statistics** and **Frequency Distribution** with either SPSS or GB-STAT. You will notice that GB-STAT calculates the mean automatically but that with SPSS you must select **Statistics** from the frequency window and select the measures desired. Select **Continue,** then **OK,** and the result will be the addition of the three measures of central tendency (mean = 260.91; median = 245; mode = 265).

Caution in Interpretation

Continuing to use our Westside High School math scores as an example, we are tempted to feel pretty good about our students and their mean score of 261 (260.91)—that is a respectable achievement score. But we need to be careful about assuming that the whole class did well on their math assessment. Look closely at Table 3.4 and the frequency distribution in relationship to the mean score of 261.

Yes, we can feel pleased that 66 of our students scored at or above the average of 260.91. But there is serious cause for alarm when noticing that a greater number (69) of our high school students scored well below the average of 260.91, with specifically 28 students at the very bottom of our distribution. These 28 students didn't seem to affect the mean so much because there was a corresponding number of 26 students who scored very high on our distribution (301-312). Now data-driven decision making must kick in. What can we do about those 28 students? Could any instructional decisions help raise their scores? Are they perhaps limited-English-speaking students who need additional help in the area of language?

The problem with using the mean to fully describe our group is that the measure does not take into account the spread or range of scores. It does not tell us how our scores are spread out from the mean or how tightly they are centered on the mean. Remember, the calculation of the mean is an average. Would it help us to know the mean along with some other measure of spread or variability? Yes, and probably the most important measure to take into consideration when looking at student achievement is the standard deviation.

TABLE 3.4 Westside Students' Math Achievement

Score	Frequency
230	14
235	14
236	13
240	14
245	14
260.91 (Mean)	(Not a specific score)
265	27
287	13
301	13
312	13
Total	135

NOTE: Standard deviation = 27.94.

Measures of Variability

Measures of variability provide quantitative measures of the degree to which the scores are spread out or clustered together. With our math scores at Westside High School, knowing that the mean score is 261 is important. But would we not also like to know how many high scores and low scores are present? And how high and how low? Though there are several measures of variability (range, interquartile range, variance, standard deviation), the standard deviation is the most commonly used and most important measure of variability.

The standard deviation uses the mean as a reference point and measures variability by considering the distance between each score and the mean. Simply, it is an approximate average of all the individual differences between each score and the mean. It is beyond the scope of this book to discuss the equations for calculating the standard deviation. Remember, GB-STAT and SPSS can do it for us. However, it is important to understand the standard deviation conceptually. Perhaps an illustration is in order. Think of the standard deviation as a number that helps us describe the middle 68%, represented by 1 unit below the mean and 1 unit above the mean (these are called Z scores, but that is not necessary to know now). Let's return to our Westside High School math scores and ask SPSS or GB-STAT to calculate a standard deviation. When selecting **Frequency Distribution,** we select **Statistics** and check standard deviation. This time, SPSS reports a standard deviation of 27.94 along with the frequency distribution. Table 3.5 helps illustrate the additional information we now have regarding our high school test scores. Subtracting the standard deviation of 27.94 from our mean gives us 233, and adding 27.94 to our mean gives us 289—the spread of 68% of our student scores.

Let's suppose the standard deviation is 52. The majority (68%) of our student scores will then range from 208 to 312. Wow! The scores are really spread out all over the place. As another example, let's suppose the standard deviation is 2. The majority of our student scores will now range only from 258 to 262. Now that's a different story! Most of our students scored very close to the mean of 260 and are stacked very close to the mean.

With our knowledge of measures of central tendency and variability, we can move on to looking at more school data and learning how to make wise data-driven decisions about student achievement. In Chapter 4, we begin to look at more strategies to help us describe and explain the data we have in our schools. We also will begin to answer some of the questions that the principal Michael Johnston asked in the beginning of this chapter: Is there perhaps a relationship between student test scores and socioeconomic status? Is there possibly a relationship between how students perform in math and how they perform in language? Can the data analysis help convince our teachers to do more collaborative teaching across grade levels and subject areas? In Chapter 4, we will discuss one of the most common procedures that educators can use to interpret school data. The procedure, called *hypothesis testing,* can help us as we make decisions about appropriate and effective instructional strategies.

Conclusion

Doesn't it seem as if we always hear the term *average*? We talk about the "average student," the "average teacher's salary," and even the "average

TABLE 3.5 Westside Students' Math Achievement, Showing Standard Deviation (Bracketed)

Scores	Frequency
230	14
235	14
236	13
240	14
245	14
260.91	Mean
265	27
287	13
301	13
312	13

NOTE: Standard deviation = approximately 68% of the scores between 232 and 289.

Joe." A measure of central tendency is the most common and most descriptive statistic we use. Generally, it is the single most important description of a sample, population, or distribution.

The *mean* is the most widely used measure both in our everyday communication and in serious research studies. The mean is the preferred choice because it is affected by each individual score or number. The *median* simply is the 50th percentile of the distribution and is the exact midpoint of the total number of scores. As you can conclude, the disadvantage of the median as a descriptive measure is that it does not reflect an extreme score such as a perfect score or that one "million-dollar home." The *mode* is the most frequently occurring score or number in the distribution and is not especially valuable to know or as reliable as the mean and median.

As measures of central tendency describe the average or most representative score in a distribution, measures of variability get at the issue of the magnitude of the differences among the scores. In other words, how spread out or how close together are the individual scores? You can imagine the importance of knowing whether a class of math exam scores ranged from 15 to 99 or from 65 to 99. Though there are several measures of variability, the range, variance, and standard deviation are the most common and valuable. And of these three, the standard deviation is most important to us in our work in schools. Hopefully, you see the importance of both measures of central tendency and variability.

Application Activities

1. Would there ever be a situation in which all three measures of central tendency in a distribution of student test scores would be the same number? Why or why not? If so, what could you say about the group of students with regard to their performance?

2. The mean salary for teachers in Idaho is $32,000, and the median salary is $28,000. Draw a distribution curve representing the state's teachers, and comment on why the median salary is lower than the mean salary.

4 Introduction to Hypothesis Testing

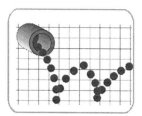

Before you allow the statistics terminology to scare you off, permit me to explain why educators might be interested in testing hypotheses. I suggest that we ask the kinds of questions every day that lend themselves to hypothesis testing. First of all, a hypothesis can help educators differentiate between real patterns in the data and patterns that may happen just by chance. For example, do students perform better in math if they have supplemental experiences with manipulatives, or do higher scores just result by chance? The goal of hypothesis testing is to decide whether the results indicate a real relationship between two variables or whether the results are happening just by chance. For example, our third-grade teacher Karla in Chapter 1 had reason to suspect that her district's current math curriculum was not benefiting both her lower and her higher academic students. She could not prove the suspicion, but she really felt there was a pattern surfacing over the years with her third-grade students. Let's help Karla create two kinds of hypotheses:

Null Hypothesis: The third-grade students in Karla's math class who rank below average and those who rank above average in math scores will show no difference (null) in their rates of math achievement over a 4-year period.

Alternative Hypothesis: The third-grade students in Karla's math class who rank below average and those who rank above average in math scores

will show a significant difference in their rates of math achievement over a
4-year period.

To help understand the hypothesis structure, you might think of how
our court system tries suspected criminals. Take, for example, the famous
O.J. Simpson case of a few years ago. The defense presented a *null hypothesis:* There is no guilt, no difference, the defendant is innocent. The prosecution, on the other hand, presented an *alternative hypothesis*: enough evidence exists to suspect that there is guilt, a difference, and the defendant is
guilty. In this case, the jury decided the evidence warranted a rejection of the
alternative hypothesis and an acceptance of the null hypothesis.

Karla presented enough evidence (test scores) from her third-grade
classroom to indicate that the higher-level students in her class were achieving at a slower rate than the lower-level students in math.

In all hypothesis testing, there is danger of making an incorrect decision. As we will learn shortly, there is a procedure we can use to reduce and
hopefully minimize the chance of making the wrong decision. Hypothesis
testing (and data-driven decision making) can be summed up in four simple
steps:

1. State the null and alternative hypotheses.

2. Decide on the criterion for a decision—how much of a difference is
   significant?

3. Collect your data and analyze.

4. Make a decision.

Z Scores

Covering Step 1 was easy as we found out in Karla's case study, but
Step 2 requires familiarity with Z scores. Hang on, we will go slow! It really
is pretty simple. Reflecting back on our Westside High School test scores,
recall that we had a set of data with a mean score of 261 (260.91). The individual test scores were considerably spread out. Wouldn't it be nice if we
could come up with a system of transforming all those scores into a few sim-

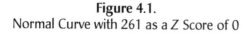

Figure 4.1.
Normal Curve with 261 as a *Z* Score of 0

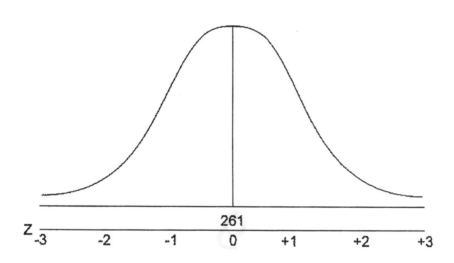

ple numbers? Displayed in Figure 4.1 is a strategy for transforming all Westside math test scores into something called *Z* scores.

The mean of your set of scores (sample) is always transformed to zero. Values above the mean are +1, +2, +3, and higher; values below the mean are –1, –2, –3, and lower. Because numbers are continuous, *Z* scores also fall between the numbers as decimals. As an example, a score of 265 (slightly higher than the mean of 261) will fall at approximately .30 as a *Z* score. Conversely, a score of 259 (slightly lower than the mean of 261) might be represented by a *Z* score of –.25.

A Note About the Distribution Curve

You will notice that in all of the figures displaying a distribution curve, as the distance from the mean increases, the ends or tails of the curve never actually touch the horizontal axis. This is because a theoretical distribution has an infinite range. Though Figure 4.1 (and others) might show a *Z* score range only from –3 to +3, there are actually Z scores further out the tail of the curve and beyond 3. Don't let a Z score of 3.9 fool you!

Why Are Z Scores Useful?

Suppose John, a Westside High School student, scored 289 in his math examination. How did he do? All that we can determine is that he scored somewhere above the mean of 261. But depending on the overall spread of the group, 289 may not be that impressive. We need more information—the mean itself is not enough to tell John the exact location of his score.

Remember our discussion of standard deviation in Chapter 3? And remember our brief mention of standard deviation as a number that represents a unit of measure? A Z score of 1 is one of those units. So are 2 and 3 and all decimals (e.g., 2.3) in between. *Oops!* So are –1, –2, and –3 (and decimals in between). Positive Z scores represent locations above the mean, and negative Z scores represent locations below the mean.

The standard deviation of our Westside math scores is 28 (27.94). This number represents one standard deviation unit (+1 above the mean and –1 below the mean). So the mean (261) plus 28 points (289) falls on a Z score of +1 (above the mean). The mean (261) minus 28 points (233) falls on a Z score of –1 (below the mean). John's score of 289 has a Z score of +1. As shown in Figure 4.2, this helps us pinpoint the exact location of his specific score.

$$Z = \frac{student\ score - mean}{deviation} = \frac{289 - 261}{28} = \frac{28}{28} = 1$$

The numerator in the equation measures the distance between the score and the mean and indicates whether the score is above (+) or below (–) the mean. We divide this distance by the standard deviation because we want the Z score to measure distance in terms of standard deviation units. Recall that the purpose of a Z score is to specify the exact location in the distribution. This formula calculates the direction (+ or –) and the distance from the mean.

We also know that all of the scores falling between one standard deviation unit below the mean (233) and one standard deviation unit above the mean (289) represent approximately 68% of the entire sample of scores. If

Figure 4.2.
Standard Deviation and *Z* Scores

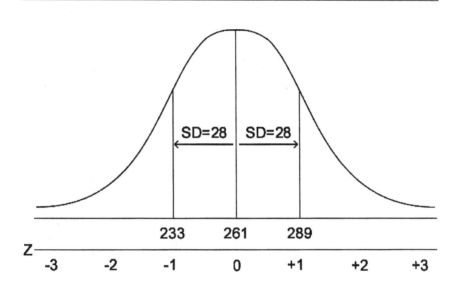

this is not real clear, hang in there—we will talk more about *Z* scores in a moment.

When we do hypothesis testing, we use data from a sample to test our alternative hypothesis. Our data will give us evidence or reason to either accept or reject the null hypothesis. If there is a *significant discrepancy* between our data and the null hypothesis (no difference), we have support for accepting our alternative hypothesis. Think again for a moment about the Simpson case. The jury decided that there was not a *significant discrepancy* between the prosecution's evidence and the null hypothesis (not guilty), so they rejected the alternative hypothesis and accepted the null hypothesis.

But how do we decide what constitutes a reason to accept or reject? Our job in Step 2 is to create a logical criterion for making this decision. Our data (sample) must be so different and represent such a significant discrepancy from the normal population that we are justified in making a decision in favor of our alternative hypothesis. If we cannot show a significant difference, then we are not justified in accepting our alternative hypothesis and therefore must accept the null hypothesis. If we accept without enough evidence, we are guilty of making a serious error (called Type II error). Some might argue that this type of error was made in the Simpson case. While we are on the subject, you might guess correctly that Type I error occurs when you reject the null hypothesis when it is actually true. More on this later, perhaps.

Z scores, in combination with what are called *probability values* or *alpha levels,* will enable us to determine what constitutes a significant difference. Let's take time out and look at an example.

As superintendent of the Westside School District, I have a suspicion that our graduating seniors have a significantly higher grade point average (GPA) than the average senior in Fresno County, California. If this is true, the difference in GPA between our seniors and the county's average must be significantly different for me to be justified in calling the local paper to publicize our success. The real question is: How different do the GPAs have to be? This gets us to Step 2—setting the criterion for making a decision. First, let me complete Step I and state the null and alternative hypotheses:

Null Hypothesis: There is no significant difference between Westside seniors' GPA and the Fresno County average.

Alternative Hypothesis: There is a significant difference between Westside seniors' GPA and the Fresno County average.

To be justified in rejecting the null and accepting the alternative, I must show considerable evidence and significant difference in the GPAs. If our seniors' GPA average (mean) is only a few points higher, the critics will say that it could have happened by chance. Just a coincidence, they will say!

I must determine what constitutes a low probability of chance as opposed to a high probability of chance. This specific probability value is a statistical term called *level of significance* or the *alpha level.* In education, we use two common probability values: .05 and .01. Simply, .05 means that there are only 5 chances out of 100 that our data resulted from chance. A

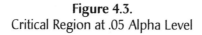

Figure 4.3.
Critical Region at .05 Alpha Level

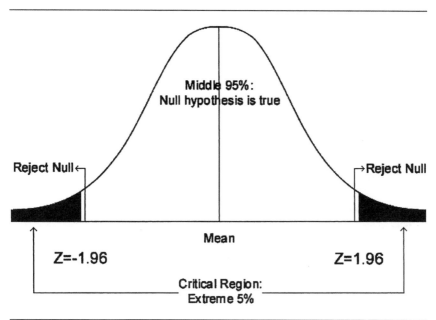

more significant probability level is .01, meaning that there is only 1 chance out of 100 that our data resulted from chance. You can see that if we set our criterion at .01 we can be more certain that our alternative hypothesis is true and will risk less chance of error in our decision. However, it can also be argued that meeting the .01 level is much harder than meeting a .05 level.

These extremely unlikely levels (.01 and .05), along with a statistic called the Z score, will help us identify what are called *critical regions*. If our data fall in these critical regions, they will be inconsistent with the null hypothesis and will lend support for our argued difference in higher GPAs. Whenever our sample data produce a mean score that is so different from the population mean that it falls in the critical region of the distribution, we can reject the null hypothesis and accept the alternative hypothesis.

Figure 4.3 shows how Z scores and alpha levels are used together to determine the critical region. If your sample mean falls at or beyond the Z score of—1.96 or +1.96 at a probability level of .05, your sample falls in the critical region and therefore allows you to accept your alternative

Figure 4.4.
Critical Region for $Z = 1.4$

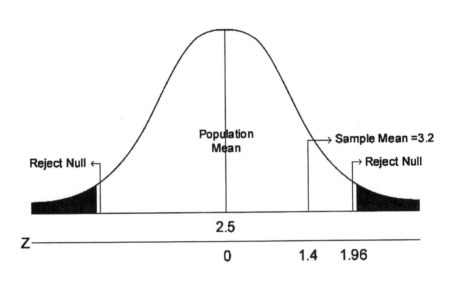

hypothesis. The sample is different enough and shows a significant discrepancy between the normal population and the sample that you can justify the decision to reject the null hypothesis and accept the alternative hypothesis.

If, on the other hand, the sample mean corresponds to a Z score of less than the 1.96, the difference is not enough to be significant and does not warrant a decision to reject the null—on the contrary, in this case the null must be retained. In addition, there are more than 5 out of 100 chances that the result happened by chance.

Let's go back to my hypothesis that Westside seniors have significantly higher GPAs than the population average (mean). Suppose the population (Fresno County) mean GPA is 2.5 with a standard deviation of 0.5. Westside seniors have a mean GPA of 3.2. We first of all know that the sample mean is higher than the population mean, but the real question is: Does the difference show a significant discrepancy, and is the difference great enough that we can say that the result is significant with fewer than 5 chances out of 100 happening by chance (alpha level = .05)? Figure 4.4 shows our sample mean of 3.2 transformed into a Z score of 1.4 along with the critical regions for .05 alpha level. I have included the formula and calculation of the Z score.

$$Z = \frac{\text{sample mean} - \text{population mean}}{\text{standard deviation of the population}} = \frac{3.2 - 2.5}{.5} = \frac{.7}{.5} = 1.4$$

Our sample mean of 3.2 (Z score of 1.4) does not fall in the extreme 5% of critical region, so it is not different enough for me to accept my alternative hypothesis. Though Westside seniors' mean GPA is higher than the county's mean, the difference is not significant. In essence, the difference could have resulted from chance. Doing some quick math in your head probably tells you that our seniors would need a mean of 3.5 (Z score of 2.0) to fall into the critical region and thus be different enough to reject the null and accept the alternative hypothesis. You may also see that if the standard deviation were smaller (less spread out)—for example, 0.3 instead of 0.5— the resulting Z score would be 2.3, high enough to fall into the critical region at or beyond 1.9. (Excuse me while I contact my secretary and have her cancel that phone call to the *Fresno Bee,* making my somewhat premature announcement.)

The *t* Statistic

Before introducing the *t* statistic, let's recap a bit regarding our procedure for using the Z score method for testing a hypothesis. The procedure involved (a) the assumption that the sample mean and the population mean would be similar, (b) the use of standard error to determine how much difference between the two means could be expected just by chance, and (c) the calculation of a Z score to determine if the obtained result would be significantly greater than would be expected by chance. In our Westside GPA example, if the resulting Z score fell within the middle 95% of the distribution, it was not significant enough to occur by chance. On the other hand, if the resulting Z score fell at or above the critical region (+ or −1.96), the sample was significantly different and was not likely (.05) to have occurred by chance. Recall that the alpha level of .05 means that the result would occur by chance 5 or fewer times out of 100.

So we may wonder: If the Z score method works in testing a hypothesis, why the need for this thing called *t* statistic? The answer is really quite simple. To calculate a Z score, we must know the standard deviation (or variance) of the population. In our previous GPA example, the population standard deviation for the county was 0.5. But in most cases we do not know the standard deviation of the population. Without the standard deviation, we cannot compute the standard error and cannot calculate the amount of expected difference between the sample mean and the population mean.

When the population standard deviation is absent, the t statistic is used instead of the Z score. In actuality, the t statistic allows us to *estimate* the standard error of the population by using the sample standard deviation—providing an estimate of the distance between the sample mean and the population mean. Again, it is beyond the scope of this chapter to present the formula for calculating the t statistic. With the help of a t-statistical table (Resource A) and GB-STAT or SPSS, the calculation of the t statistic is quite simple.

Before we work with a real-life situation, we need to touch lightly on the concept of *degrees of freedom*. Degrees of freedom (*df*) is a number that describes the number of values (scores) that are free to vary in that distribution (sample). To simplify, suppose you have a distribution of three scores and you know that the sum is 30. If you assign two of the three values—10 and 15—the third value is not free to vary because it must be 5 to achieve the sum of 30. Given the two values, 10 + 15 = 25, and the sum of 30, the third value must equal 5. The point is that the third value is not free to vary. Just remember, the *df* for a distribution of a sample variable is equal to the sample number minus 1. In our Westside GPA example, *df* = 19 (20−1). The practical implication for using degrees of freedom is that reducing the sample size by 1 results in a smaller t value, reducing the risk of underestimating the standard error. This is particularly the case with small sample sizes. As you can guess, the greater the value of *df* for a distribution, the closer the sample variance represents the population variance, and the better the t statistic approximates the Z score. No surprise here—the larger the sample, the more accurate our decision to reject or accept the hypothesis.

One-Sample *t* Test: An Example

We return to our Westside seniors and will use a t statistic rather than a Z score to test the alternate hypothesis that our GPA mean score is significantly different from the county average. To simplify the procedure, let's use

TABLE 4.1 Westside GPA Scores

Student	GPA	Student	GPA
1	2.5	11	3.3
2	2.8	12	2.9
3	2.6	13	2.4
4	2.9	14	2.3
5	2.4	15	2.5
6	2.5	16	2.7
7	2.7	17	2.5
8	2.9	18	2.8
9	3.1	19	2.9
10	3.2	20	3.0

a small sample of 20 seniors. Table 4.1 displays their GPA scores. Take a moment and create your own file titled "Westside *t*-Statistics" using the data in Table 4.1.

Let's follow the four steps mentioned earlier in this chapter.

1. *State the null and alternative hypotheses.*

   Null: The mean GPA of Westside seniors is not significantly different from the county average of 2.5.

   Alternative: The mean GPA of Westside seniors is significantly different from the county average of 2.5.

2. *Decide on a criterion for a decision.* We will identify the critical region of the distribution where our sample mean must fall to be significant. Selecting an alpha level of .05, we look at Resource A to determine the critical *t* value associated with 19 degrees of freedom ($N-1$). This value is 2.09 for an alpha level of .05. We will compare the observed sample *t* value to the critical value of 2.09.

3. *Analyze the data.* You must trust that I correctly calculated the observed *t* value of our Westside sample to be 3.89. We will turn to GB-STAT in a minute to see if my calculation agrees.

4. *Make a decision.* From Step 2 above, we recall that for our sample data to be statistically significant, the obtained *t* value must be 2.09 or greater. In this case, the observed *t* value of 3.89 is greater than the critical value (2.09), so we can reject the null and accept our alternative hypothesis—that our seniors' GPA is significantly higher than the county average.

Using GB-STAT and SPSS for the *t* Test of Hypotheses

Open your newly created file titled "Westside *t*-Statistic." For this *t* test, we will use GB-STAT followed by SPSS.

GB-STAT

After "Westside *t*-Statistic" is opened, select **Statistics** from the main menu, then **Student T-Tests,** followed by **One Sample.** Select *GPA* as the variable (double-click), and type in the county average of 2.5 under the selection **Compare to What?** The population (county) is 2.5. Select **Go,** and the *t* test as displayed in Table 4.2 will appear.

SPSS

After "Westside *t*-Statistic" is opened, select **Statistics** (in Version 8.0) or **Analyze** (in Version 9.0) on the menu bar, and then select **Compare Means.** Choose a **One-Sample T-Test,** highlight the variable *GPA,* and move to the right side of the screen. You will notice that the Test Value box defaults to 0. Type 2.5 (population mean) in this box, and select **OK.** The result of the *t* test is displayed in Table 4.3.

You will first notice that SPSS prints out some descriptive statistics such as sample number, mean, and standard deviation. The box below the descriptive information displays the significance of the *t* test. Mean differ-

TABLE 4.2 GB-STAT One-Sample *t* Test for GPA

Sample Name	GPA
Sample mean	2.745
Standard deviation	0.2819
Standard error	0.063
Comparison value	2.5
t value	3.887
Degrees of freedom	19
Probability	0.001

TABLE 4.3 SPSS One-Sample *t* Test for GPA

	One-Sample Statistics		
	N	Mean	SD
GPA	20	2.74	.2819

	One-Sample Test (Test Value = 2.5)		
	t	*df*	Sig.	Mean Diff.
GPA	3.887	19	.001	.2450

ence is the difference between the observed sample mean (2.745) and the population mean (2.5). The important question: Is a mean difference of .2450 large enough to be significantly different from 2.5? The results of the *t* test reveal that $t = 3.88$, with 19 ($N - 1$) degrees of freedom (*df*). The two-tailed significance (.001) shows an alpha level less than our chosen .05. We can reject the null and accept the alternative for a couple of reasons: (a) The *t* value of 3.88 is well into the critical region of 2.09 (selected from the *t*-statistical table in Appendix A), and (b) the test is significant at an even lower alpha level than the one we chose (.001).

Conclusion

Both the Z-score and the *t*-statistic tests are used to test hypotheses between sample and population data. The reason for using the *t* test in most instances relates to the information that we do not usually have (the population variance). The *t* test allows us to analyze data when we have little information about the population. The real advantage of the *t* test is that we can test our alternative hypothesis with just a null hypothesis and a sample from a perhaps little-known population.

With the enormous amount of school data we collect (and most often have stored on a shelf someplace), such as standardized and criterion-referenced test scores, average daily attendance (ADA), grades, and dropout figures, the *t* statistic lends itself very nicely to improving the decision-making process through the use of data. In Chapter 5, we will learn how to use this same *t* statistic with more than one sample—the independent-samples *t* test. Again, both GB-STAT and SPSS will simplify the procedure and continue to make our lives easier. Analyzing data is one thing—saving time in our professional lives to make wise instructional decisions about teaching and learning is quite another.

Application Activities

1. As a sixth-grade teacher, you are concerned about the prealgebra test that your class must take at the end of the year in preparation for seventh grade. Their performance determines placement in prealgebra or general math. The district scores for students placed in prealgebra over the last several years reveal a mean score of 92 and a standard deviation of 4. After several weeks of preparation, you administer a practice test to your sixth graders. The result is a mean score of 94. Is the mean difference significant enough to lead you to believe that your class is ready to pass the prealgebra test in May?

2. An article in *Education Week* reports the findings of a study with 21 degrees of freedom. How many people participated in the study? Did the researcher use a Z statistic or a t statistic? For what reason was the selected test used?

3. Many of us as teachers say we grade our students "on a curve." What does this really mean? In what ways are measures of central tendency and variability related to this practice?

5 The Independent-Samples *t* Test

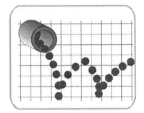

Much of what we want to know in education involves two samples rather than one. For instance, we often want to compare two methods of instruction, such as phonics instruction versus the whole-language approach. Do students learn science better or faster if they are exposed to instruction in the field as opposed to others receiving instruction only in the traditional classroom setting? Do limited-English-speaking students who receive English as a second language (ESL) instruction become more efficient English speakers than limited-English speakers who do not receive ESL instruction? As you can guess, most research studies involve the comparison of two (or more) sets of data. Sometimes our sample is the same, but we are exposing the same number of students to two different methods of instruction, which in fact gives us two separate data sets. These kinds of studies are called independent-measures research designs, meaning that they analyze the mean difference between the two samples. The statistical test used in this kind of study is also called the independent-measures *t* statistic. More on this later.

Remember how we talked about the difference between a mean of a sample and the mean of a population? We also, especially with the Z-score method, compared the standard error of the sample and population. The result of our testing looked very closely at the differences between the means and standard errors of the sample and population.

If we are now going to look at two independent samples, can you see that we probably will be interested in looking at these same items between the two independent samples? So we are really looking at something like the following:

The mean of one sample compared to the mean of another sample compared to the population mean—then all of this related to the standard error of one sample compared to the standard error of the other sample

Again, we will not get into the formula, but actually the formula was just stated above in words. Hopefully, you have a general conceptual idea of what happens in an independent-samples *t* test. The following example may help.

A Personal Hypothesis

Allow me to share a personal story and how perhaps we can use the independent-samples *t* statistic to test my hypothesis. Three years ago, I taught a course called "Applied Quantitative Methods" (a fancy term for applied educational statistics) to teacher education majors at the University of Wyoming. My instruction was delivered in a very traditional classroom setting, focusing primarily on the textbook. Most of the examples used were not from the field of education but from psychology and other social sciences. I still have in my files records of their final examinations.

Two years ago, I accepted a position at Idaho State University, and I currently teach a similar course to aspiring and practicing teachers and principals. But my instructional delivery has changed dramatically. I now use examples specific to the classroom and request students to bring their collected data sets from their schools. Though we use a textbook, it serves as more of a guide as we roll up our sleeves and mess with data from our workplace.

Step 1: Stating the Hypotheses

I am beginning to sense that my present students are attaining higher grades on their final exams. Perhaps this is because of my increased years of experience with teaching this course, but I want to test the hypothesis that my students at Idaho State University are achieving at a higher level than my previous students at the University of Wyoming due to a different instructional delivery method. Allow me to follow Step 1 and set up my null and alternative hypotheses.

> Null: There is no significant difference between the academic achievement (as measured by a final examination) of students at the University of Wyoming (UW) and those at Idaho State University (ISU).

> Alternative: The sample means for the two groups of students (UW and ISU) are not equal and are therefore significantly different due to a different instructional strategy.

I suspect my friends from Laramie will not be happy with my alternative hypothesis, but I will press forward with my thinking. I have taken a random sample of 20 students from each of the two universities. Their final exam scores appear in Table 5.1. Time to test your skills again. Create a file titled "Independent Samples." Label your columns as follows: column 1, Students 1-40; column 2, ISU or UW; column 3, Exam Score.

Step 2: Deciding on the Criterion for Making a Decision

Before I check the t-statistic table in Resource A to identify the critical region and alpha level, let me point out that in this case there will be two separate degrees of freedom (df). Can you guess why? Correct—because there are two independent samples, we will have $(n - 1) + (n - 1)$. There is one score in each sample that is not free to vary. So, with degrees of freedom of 38 and an alpha level of .05, Resource A indicates a critical region of approximately 2.03 (between 30 and 40). For me to reject the null of no difference in means between my two classes, the observed t value of the two samples must be 2.03 or greater to be in the critical region of rejection. Figure 5.1 helps clarify.

One-Tailed Versus Two-Tailed Test

Please note that the critical region is identified at both a positive t value and a negative t value. This represents a two-tailed test. It is necessary in this analysis because I am not sure that my ISU students will score higher (2.3 or higher)—they may score lower. That is why my hypothesis states a differ-

TABLE 5.1 Final Exam Scores for Idaho State University (ISU) and University of Wyoming (UW) Sample Students

Student	University	Score	Student	University	Score
1	ISU	85	21	UW	80
2	ISU	93	22	UW	70
3	ISU	87	23	UW	93
4	ISU	72	24	UW	58
5	ISU	71	25	UW	85
6	ISU	90	26	UW	85
7	ISU	61	27	UW	87
8	ISU	88	28	UW	84
9	ISU	92	29	UW	74
10	ISU	82	30	UW	72
11	ISU	89	31	UW	83
12	ISU	88	32	UW	72
13	ISU	73	33	UW	88
14	ISU	91	34	UW	89
15	ISU	85	35	UW	86
16	ISU	83	36	UW	61
17	ISU	88	37	UW	68
18	ISU	87	38	UW	70
19	ISU	85	39	UW	82
20	ISU	83	40	UW	58

ence and does not indicate a direction. Perhaps they will fall significantly lower and fall in the negative critical region (−2.03 or below).

Step 3: Analyzing the Data

Again, you must trust that I correctly calculated (with formula) the observed *t* value to be 2.06. A bit later, we will bring GB-STAT and SPSS to the rescue.

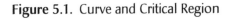

Figure 5.1. Curve and Critical Region

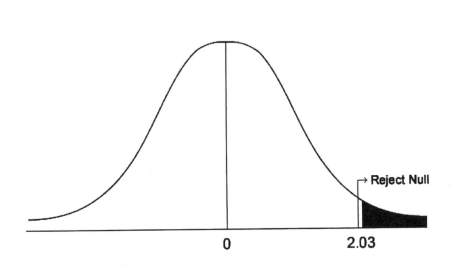

Step 4: Making a Decision

The observed *t* value for my samples is 2.06, just a tad higher than the critical value of 2.03 (Wow! pretty close). I reject the null hypothesis at the .05 level of significance.

Using GB–STAT and SPSS
for Independent Samples

Open the file you just created, titled "Independent Samples." After opening GB-STAT or SPSS, select **File,** then **Open Data File,** and then **Independent Samples.** As before, both GB-STAT and SPSS will be explained in the next section.

SPSS

After the ISU file is open, select **Statistics** (Version 8) or **Analyze** (Version 9), and then choose **Compare Means**. This time select **Independent Samples t-Test.**

Oops! Another discussion item. You will be asked to select an *independent variable.* Let me suggest that you just memorize the following, as I have had to do (and still get them confused occasionally). The independent variable is one that is manipulated or changed—in this case, the university or teaching style was manipulated or changed. The *dependent variable* is something that all members of the sample receive equally—in this case, each of the 40 university students received a final examination. Any kind of test or measurement is a dependent variable if it is consistently administered to both samples. The treatment or different instructional strategy will represent the independent variable.

You will need to move the final exam variable to the Test Variable box on the right side of the screen (single-click on the exam and move to the right with the highlighted arrow). You will then need to move the independent variable to the Grouping Variable box. The term *grouping variable* should help with the definition because you will "group" the university variable—some ISU and others UW. After you move the variable *University Attended* to the Grouping Variable box, you will notice the **Define Group** button highlighted. You must now tell SPSS how you want your groups defined. Simply select **Define Groups** and type in "ISU" for Group 1 and "UW" for Group 2. Click on **Continue,** then **OK** from original *t*-test screen.

Clicking on **Continue** from the Define Groups box and then **OK** from the original *t*-test screen results in your independent-samples *t*-test analysis, shown in Table 5.2.

As we noticed in the one-sample analysis, SPSS first gives you the descriptive data (e.g., number, means, standard deviation, and standard error) on the dependent variable (final exam) for each of the two university samples (ISU and UW). We will not deal with the Levine's test for equality of variance in this book. A bit to the right, you will see "t-test for equality of means"—that's us. Back to the left of the output screen you notice "Equal variances assumed" and "Equal variances not assumed." For our work, we will disregard the row "Equal variances not assumed" because we really suspect that our variances between university classes are the same or similar.

TABLE 5.2 SPSS *t*-Test Analysis of Final Exam Scores for ISU
and UW Students

| University Attended | N | Group Statistics | | |
		Mean	SD	Std. Error Mean
Final exam				
ISU	20	83.65	8.24	1.84
UW	20	77.40	10.81	2.42

| | Independent-Samples Test | | | |
| | t Test for Equality of Means | | | |
	t	*df*	*Sig.*	*Mean Diff.*
Final exam (equal variances assumed)	2.057	38	.047	6.25

SPSS uses a procedure called "pooled variance estimate" to combine the two sample variances to obtain the most accurate estimate of the variance common to both classes.

Our obvious *t* value for the ISU/UW samples is 2.057, with degrees of freedom ($n - 1$ for each of the two samples) equal to 38. The two-tailed probability of .047 is less than our selection of .05, which allows us to consider the test significant and allows us to reject the null hypothesis of no difference at the .05 alpha level.

GB-STAT

After the ISU file is open, select **Statistics,** then **Student t-Tests** and **Two Sample t-Test.** GB-STAT will ask if subsets are in one column—select **Subsets of One Column** because all 40 entries are entered in one column. You must then select **Dependent Variable** (final exam) and **Group Code Variable** (university) by double-clicking on each. Be certain that the value for Subset 1 equals 1 and that the value for Subset 2 equals 2. Select **OK,** and the two-sample *t* test appears and is displayed in Table 5.3.

TABLE 5.3 GB-STAT Two–Sample *t*-Test Analysis of Final Exam Scores for ISU and UW Students

Subset	1	2
Size	20	20
Mean	83.65	77.4
SD	8.24	10.80

t value	2.0566
df	38
Two-tailed probability	0.0466

GB-STAT also displays the means and standard deviations of each sample. Notice the obtained *t* value of 2.0566, the 38 degrees of freedom, and the two-tailed probability of .0466. GB-STAT confirms our decision to reject the null hypothesis at the .05 level of significance.

A Caution

As was the case in this *t* test, the significance was very close (2.03 vs. 2.06). Though the *t*-statistic rule states *at or beyond* the critical *t* value, you can see that if one or two more ISU students had attained a slightly lower score, the sample might have resulted in a lower observed *t* value, thus falling below the critical *t* value. I need to be careful at this point about making judgments about my two different teaching strategies. The result certainly gives me reason to suspect a difference, but perhaps another study (with two larger samples) might be in order. Oh, well! I suspect my friends in Laramie feel a little better after finding the difference so close.

Okay, Your Turn Now

Let's try another example more closely related to your role as an educator. All of us continue to struggle with the problems of the limited-English speaker in our schools as languages other than English spoken in our classrooms continue to increase. My friend and colleague Ed is a principal in an

TABLE 5.4 Reading Scores of Students With and Without English as a
Second Language (ESL) Program

Student	ESL	Student	No ESL
1	35	11	29
2	29	12	26
3	37	13	35
4	32	14	32
5	21	15	20
6	28	16	25
7	35	17	30
8	32	18	29
9	31	19	22
10	30	20	24

elementary school in the Santa Ana Unified School District. His district administrators feel so strongly about offering English as a second language (ESL) as a way of helping the limited-English speaker adapt that they designate Ed's elementary school as a magnet school for K-3 students who speak English as a second language.

Ed is interested in determining if students in his school become English proficient (better or faster) than limited-English speakers in the general population of his district. He decides to compare a sample of third graders from his elementary school with a sample of third graders (limited-English speakers) from other schools in his district where ESL is not used as an instructional strategy. As best can be determined, his samples account for such factors as similar number of years spent in public schools. Both samples take an English proficiency assessment measuring reading ability. Table 5.4 displays scores from both groups.

Using the data shown in Table 5.4, create a file titled "ESL Sample." Let's determine if there is a significant effect of ESL instruction (as measured by a proficiency test) with third-grade limited-English students in Ed's district. Students from Ed's elementary school are grouped as 1, and the sample from the district at large is coded as 2. Use the independent-samples *t* test to test the null hypothesis that there is no difference in the mean scores between students receiving ESL instruction and those who do not. Use the .05 level of significance. Obviously, Ed's alternative hypothesis is that there is a statistically significant difference between the two groups.

Take a well-deserved break from my writing, and test your computer analysis skills with either GB-STAT or SPSS. Come back in a few minutes, and we will consider Ed's hypothesis.

Break's Over—How Did Ed's Students Do?

First of all, you will notice from your data analysis that Ed's students had a mean score of 31 and the district group attained a mean of 27.2. In essence, our question is: Is the mean difference great or significant enough to allow us to reject the null hypothesis of no difference and accept Ed's alternative hypothesis that ESL instruction has a positive effect on the acquisition of English proficiency skills? Looking at our two-sample *t*-test analysis, we find an observed *t* value of 1.85 with a two-tailed probability (alpha level) of .08. We have a couple problems here: (a) The observed *t* value of 1.85 is not as great as the critical *t* value of 2.10 that we find in Resource A, and (b) the alpha level of .08 indicates more possibility of error than our selected .05. The *t* test is not considered significant at the .05 level, so we must accept the null hypothesis of no significant difference in scores and reject Ed's alternative hypothesis. Table 5.5 displays the GB-STAT two-sample *t*-test results.

Conclusion

We should not leave Ed's hypothesis so quickly! Remember, statistical analysis does not prove anything; rather, it helps us identify patterns and encourages us to ask additional questions. The responsibility of data-driven decision making is thrown back on us. Ed decides to look further at his two samples and discovers that there may be other variables at play here. For instance, perhaps there is a difference in the primary language of the parents influencing whether the child speaks English in the home. Home reading habits may vary. Ed decides to do another study.

TABLE 5.5 GB-STAT Two-Sample *t*-Test Analysis of Reading Scores and ESL Program

Subset	1 (With ESL)	2 (Without ESL)
Size	10	10
Mean	31	27.2
SD	4.52	4.638

t value	1.855	
df	18	
Two-tailed probability	0.08	

His real suspicion is that class size may be a variable—in other words, maybe he was comparing ESL instruction in a class of 30 to non-ESL instruction in a class of 20. He still believes ESL instruction is effective but also suggests that class size is an important factor. His new study will look at ESL versus non-ESL instruction but, in addition, will compare three different class sizes (small, medium, and large).

As powerful as the *t* statistic is, it has one limitation. The *t* test can be used only with one or two samples or treatments. Ed's new questions involve the comparison of more than two sample means—six, to be specific. He will have three sample means for ESL instruction (small, medium, and large) and three additional samples for non-ESL instruction (small, medium, and large).

We now need the help of something called analysis of variance (ANOVA). Wait a minute—don't leave me yet. The ANOVA sounds more complex and complicated than it really is. I promise it is no more intimidating than our work with *Z* scores a few chapters ago. Quite honestly, we are on the downhill side. Press on!

Application Activity

1. A high school math teacher feels strongly that students can learn math better outside the classroom with hands-on materials and problems.

He devises a semester course taught outside and integrating such tools as computer probe-ware, tape measures, thermometers, and measuring wheels. He is interested in determining the effect of this new course. His hypothesis is that the students taking the outdoor course will perform better than a class taught inside with the traditional instructional delivery, as measured by the annual standardized achievement test given by the district. The exam scores of 10 students receiving outside instruction and the exam scores of 10 students receiving the inside instruction are listed below. (Please note that 1 = outside class and 2 = inside class).

Student	Instruction	Score	Student	Instruction	Score
1	1	230	11	2	232
2	1	228	12	2	222
3	1	234	13	2	210
4	1	212	14	2	190
5	1	199	15	2	205
6	1	220	16	2	205
7	1	210	17	2	195
8	1	205	18	2	189
9	1	200	19	2	209
10	1	220	20	2	205

We are testing the null hypothesis that there is no statistically significant difference in student math achievement as a result of outside hands-on instruction compared to the inside traditional instruction. Using either GB-STAT or SPSS, create a data file with the information above. Conduct an independent-samples *t* test at the .05 level of significance level. Don't forget degrees of freedom.

6 Analysis of Variance

*The Difference Between
Two or More Samples*

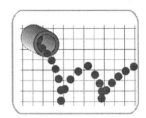

Analysis of variance (ANOVA) is a procedure for evaluating the mean differences between two or more samples. But wait a minute! Isn't that what you said about *t* tests? In a sense, the *t* test and the ANOVA are quite similar. Both tests use sample data to test hypotheses about population means.

Advantages of ANOVA
Over *t* Tests

As stated before, the real advantage of the ANOVA is the fact that it allows you to analyze two *or more* samples or treatments. A *t* test is an appropriate procedure for one or two samples but not for more than two. The ANOVA permits the educator to compare many variables at one time, allowing for much more flexibility. For instance, look at the information displayed in Table 6.1. In this instance, we are interested in looking at the effect of two treatments: phonics versus whole-language instruction. An additional question is: Are there differences between Schools A, B, and C?

Another very important advantage of the ANOVA has to do with our old friend Type I error. Recall that as we set up our *t* test, we set an alpha level of .05—meaning that we expected (and would tolerate) a 1 in 20 chance of error in our test. For a moment, suppose that we used the *t* test to analyze the data in Table 6.1. We would have to run individual *t* tests for each comparison of means. Here's the problem: A probability of error (.05)

TABLE 6.1 Introduction to ANOVA

	School A	*School B*	*School C*
Phonics instruction	Sample 1	Sample 3	Sample 5
Whole-language introduction	Sample 2	Sample 4	Sample 6

accompanies each individual test. You can see that if we made six comparisons of means, we would run a .05 chance of error six different times, causing the chance of error to rise dramatically. The ANOVA uses one test, with one alpha level to analyze the mean differences, reducing significantly the possibility of making Type I error.

Before we leave our data in Table 6.1, allow me to pose some hypothetical questions related to data-driven decision making. Suppose we found that in each of the three elementary schools, there was a significant difference (as measured by a standardized test) between phonics and whole-language instruction. Would it not be our professional and moral responsibility to closely scrutinize student achievement, instructional strategies, and assessment procedures? I believe so. Data analysis should be the basis for sound educational decision making.

Analysis of Variance

Let's start off with what seems to be an oxymoron or contradiction in terms. The formulas and calculations necessary in the ANOVA are quite complicated—but conceptually, the ANOVA is pretty simple. Wow! I got that off my chest.

First of all, take a look at the data displayed in Table 6.2. I have kept the numbers small to help with understanding. Essentially, we are testing the null hypothesis that states there is no difference in the level of computer literacy between three different sizes of class (i.e., small = 5-13; medium = 14-22; large = 23-30). A sample of five students was taken in each of the three different-size classes. The scores represent the results of a computer competency test given to all three groups after one semester of instruction.

TABLE 6.2 Scores on Computer Competency for Samples of Students From Three Differently Sized Classes

	Computer Competency Scores		
Student	Class Size 1 (Small, 5-13 Students)	Class Size 2 (Medium, 14-22 Students)	Class Size 3 (Large, 23-30 Students)
1	5	2	1
2	4	2	2
3	5	2	1
4	3	1	1
5	3	3	2
	Mean = 4	Mean = 2	Mean = 1.4

At first glance, we notice a difference favoring the small class size. But remember, our goal is to determine if the difference is significant. Perhaps it occurred by chance. The ANOVA will help us evaluate the difference—not the reason why, only whether the difference is statistically significant.

A Couple of New Terms

Before we proceed further with the ANOVA of our computer class size samples, I must introduce you to something called the F ratio. For ANOVA, the test statistic is called an F ratio as opposed to the t statistic discussed earlier. A procedural analysis of the F ratio and the t statistic may help.

$$t = \frac{difference\ between\ sample\ means}{standard\ error}$$

$$F = \frac{variance\ between\ sample\ means}{variance\ of\ the\ standard\ error}$$

You first notice that the F ratio uses the variance instead of the difference between sample means. There is a simple reason for this. Suppose you have two sample means: 22 and 32. Computing a sample mean difference is straightforward and easy to describe. However, suppose you have three sample means: 22, 32, and 41. Now describing the difference becomes more difficult, and there is really no way to calculate it. Using the variance to describe our three-sample means is much easier—the reason for the ANOVA.

A confusion to most of us involves understanding that even though the *F* ratio uses the variance in the calculation, it is used to help us evaluate the differences in the means between samples, treatments, and population. The point is that both the *t* test and the ANOVA use sample data to test hypotheses about population means. To get there, the ANOVA uses the variance in calculation.

One other term needing clarification is *mean square* or *MS*. This one is easy too—it is a term that takes the place of the variance. In statistical circles, it is common to use the term *MS* instead of *variance,* but they are the same thing. You may remember the term *sum of squares (SS)*, which defines the sum of squared deviations. We now use *mean square (MS)* to distinguish the mean of the squared deviations. This becomes important as we read the GB-STAT and SPSS report tables. More on this later.

Components of the ANOVA

Remember, the ANOVA is measuring the total amount of variability or variance. This total is composed of (a) the variance between the samples and (b) the variance within each individual sample. Reflect back for a moment to our data in Table 6.2. There is variance (and risk of error) between each of the class sizes. There is also variance (and risk of error) between the individual student scores within each of the three samples.

As I promised, I will not elaborate on the complexity of the ANOVA formulas, but I cannot resist showing you the formula in words.

$$F = \frac{variance\ between\ samples\ (treatments)}{variance\ within\ samples\ (treatments)}$$

The F Distribution

In analysis of variance, the *F* ratio is exactly that—a ratio. The numerator in the ratio is measuring the variance between groups (samples), and the

Figure 6.1. Curve of *F* Values

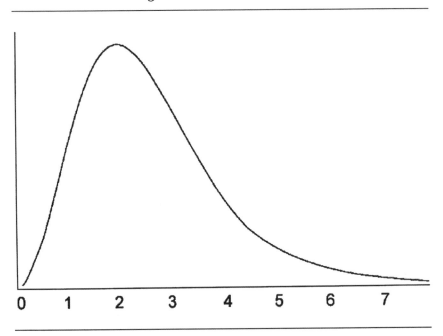

denominator is measuring variance within groups (samples). The neat thing about this distribution table (Resource B) is that we do not have to concern ourselves with negative numbers. Think for a moment. Let's suppose that the null hypothesis is true—there is no difference in the variance. For that to be true, both the numerator and denominator would approximate the same number and result in something like 1/1. If *F* values approximate 1, the null hypothesis must be accepted. So the *F*-distribution table does not go below zero, and all values are positive. Figure 6.1 may help clarify. The distribution stops at 0, is highest around 1, and then tapers off to the right.

To use the *F*-distribution table (Resource B), we must first be aware that we have two degrees of freedom, one for between groups and one for within groups. In our example in Table 6.3, our degrees of freedom (*df*) for between groups is 2 (3 classes – 1 class) and our degrees of freedom (*df*) for within groups is 12 (15 students – 3 students). Recall that we must subtract one student from each sample because they are separate and being treated alone.

Figure 6.2.
F Distribution with .05 and .01 Critical Regions

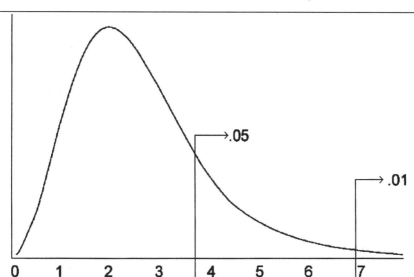

We begin looking at the *F*-distribution table by locating the number of degrees of freedom between groups (numerator) and then move down the column to find the number of degrees of freedom within groups (denominator). At this point, we find the critical value of *F* required to reject the null hypothesis of no difference between the variances. You will notice two critical values at this point: The top is the critical value for the .05 level of significance, and the bottom is the critical value for the .01 level of significance. Figure 6.2 shows that the critical region for our example of degrees of freedom equals (2, 12).

As you can see, the critical region required to reject the null of no difference is 3.88. Any value observed in our samples at 3.88 or higher gives us reason to reject the null and accept our alternative hypothesis that there is a statistically significant difference between the means of the three classes. We have arrived at another one of those "trusting moments." You must trust that my calculated *F* ratio of 15.44 is correct and well beyond the critical value of 3.88 and that it actually even meets the .01 level of significance.

GB-STAT and SPSS to the Rescue—
Checking My Calculations

Using the data found in Table 6.2, create a file in either GB-STAT or SPSS titled "Class Size Computer Instruction." If using GB-STAT, set up your file in four columns and, if SPSS, set up in three columns.

GB-STAT

Select **Statistics** and then **Analysis of Variance.** Be certain that **Completely Randomized, One-Way Design** and **Multiple Columns** are checked. If our three classes were all in one column, we would select **Subjects of One Column.** We now want to click on the button **Select Columns.**

After selecting **Select Columns,** you are asked to select your samples. In this case, we are running an ANOVA on all three samples, so we must add Class #1, Class #2, and Class #3 to the box on the right titled "Selected Samples."

After you have moved your samples to the right, choose **Done,** and the results of your ANOVA appear as displayed in Table 6.3.

As is customary with GB-STAT, some basic descriptive data are included. You notice in the printout the number of students in each sample, the mean of each sample's scores, and the number of variables being compared. Below the descriptive data, you notice the ANOVA summary table. First of all, remember that the ANOVA uses the variance as the basis for comparison rather than means and standard deviations—thus the terms *sum of squares* and *mean square.*

What we are really interested in knowing is the F ratio and the probability. Earlier, we identified the critical F ratio as anything at 3.88 or above. Our observed F ratio of 15.44 in our sample is clearly beyond that point. And to make our case even stronger, notice the probability or alpha level of .0005. The difference between our three samples is statistically significant with a very low chance of error (specifically, 5 chances in 10,000). So we are pretty safe in rejecting the null hypothesis of no difference between our three class sizes and accepting our alternative hypothesis of a difference between the three.

TABLE 6.3 GB-STAT ANOVA Summary Table for Class Size and Computer Proficiency Scores

Source	Sum of Squares	df	Mean Square	F Ratio	Probability
Between groups	18.533	2	9.2667	15.4444	0.0005
Within groups	7.2	12	0.6		
Total	25.7333	14			

SPSS

Note that in this data file I put all three classes in one column and assigned the number 1 to "small," 2 to "medium," and 3 to "large." These will be treated as subsets of one column. Select **Statistics** (Version 8) or **Analyze** (Version 9), then **Compare Means,** and then **One-Way ANOVA.** Again, as in GB-STAT, you will be asked to choose a dependent variable (test scores) and a factor or independent variable (class size). The independent variable is the one that is manipulated or changed. Do you see how we are manipulating class size? We are setting three separate conditions (class size) in which to apply our treatment (computer instruction).

Please take note of a button labeled **Post Hoc**—just note the location, as we will come back to this in a few minutes. After selecting your dependent variable and your factor (independent), select **OK.** The ANOVA summary table is displayed in Table 6.4.

As with GB-STAT, SPSS displays the sum of squares, degrees of freedom, and mean squares. Again, the F ratio is 15.44 with a significance level of .000. Keep in mind that .000 does not mean a level of zero—it means that the probability level is .0004 or less, rounded to .000. When GB-STAT reported a .0005, it revealed something in the neighborhood of .00049 rounded to .0005. GB-STAT rounds the significance level to four places beyond the decimal, whereas SPSS rounds to three places beyond the decimal.

TABLE 6.4 SPSS ANOVA Summary Table for Class Size and Computer Proficiency Scores

	Sum of Squares	df	Mean Square	F	Significance
Between groups	18.533	12	9.267	15.444	.000
Within groups	7.200	12	.600		
Total	25.733	14			

The observed F ratio of 15.44 is well beyond the critical region and above the required 3.8 at the .05 significance level. Therefore, we reject the null hypothesis of no difference and accept the alternative hypothesis of significant difference between the three class sizes.

Note that SPSS will also report descriptive statistics such as mean and standard deviation—simply select **Options** from the screen that asks for the dependent variable and factor.

Post Hoc Tests

So far, so good. Or is it? We rejected the null hypothesis of no difference between our three class sizes because of the evidence that there was truly a significant difference between the three classes. So we accepted our alternative hypothesis of a significant difference between our three computer classes. Don't we really want to know which classes were different? At this point, we do not know whether the larger class or the smaller class was more responsible for the difference. We might suspect the smaller, but we do not know that with the ANOVA results. It is not unusual for the results of an analysis to create more questions than it answers.

The results of the ANOVA did not specify which class size was most different. Is there more difference between Class Size #1 and Class Size #2 or between Class Size #2 and Class Size #3? Or are #1 and #3 perhaps similar? Post hoc tests help us answer these types of questions.

When we were using the *t* test, there was no difficulty deciding where the difference between means was—between Sample 1 and Sample 2. Obviously, there was no need for a post hoc test. However, with the ANOVA (more than two sample means), it is impossible to know which means are different.

A post hoc test can be applied to the data after the ANOVA results are calculated. If the evidence supports the acceptance of the null hypothesis, then there is no need for a post hoc test. However, if the ANOVA results in a significant difference, we can go back and compare two means at a time to determine the location of the difference. In our class size analysis, I suggest that we really want to know if the difference is more related to the smaller computer classes or the larger ones.

One of the most common post hoc tests is Tukey's HSD test. The procedure computes a single value that is related to two specific samples or treatments. This value is called the *h*onestly *s*ignificant *d*ifference.

Let's look at Tukey's HSD test to determine exactly where the difference is in our class size ANOVA. Table 6.5 displays the GB-STAT results, and Table 6.6 displays the SPSS report.

Recall that when we viewed the GB-STAT "Analysis of Variance" window earlier in this chapter, there was an option for **Multiple Comparisons.** Go back to that window and double-click on **Tukey/Kramer Procedure.** Table 6.5 is the result. Notice a matrix that correlates the three different class sizes. Again, it is beyond the scope of this book to deal with the technical formula for calculating the Tukey HSD test. When comparing Class Size #1 with Class Size #2, there is a 16.66 value of difference, significant at the .01 alpha level. That's pretty "different." Looking further, there is a 28.16 value of difference between Class Size #1 and Class Size #3 at the .01 alpha level. Wow! So most of the difference is between Class Size #1 and Class Size #3. We now have reason to suspect that students may learn computer literacy skills better and faster in a smaller class environment. Proof? No, but reason to suspect. Remember, statistical analysis does not tell us cause and effect but often provides patterns or evidence for further questions or study.

When we set up the dependent variable and factor (independent variable) in SPSS, recall that there was an optional button on the bottom of that screen titled **Post Hoc Tests.** Return to that window and select **Post Hoc Tests.** Place a check on the **Tukey,** and select **Continue.** The results are as shown in Table 6.6.

TABLE 6.5 GB-STAT Tukey/Kramer Procedure for Class Size and
Computer Proficiency Scores

	Class Size 1	Class Size 2	Class Size 3
Class Size 1	0	16.6667**	28.1667**
Class Size 2	16.6667**	0	1.5
Class Size 3	28.1667**	1.5	0

$**p < 0.01.$

TABLE 6.6 SPSS Tukey HSD for Class Size and Computer Proficiency
Scores

Class Size	Class Size	Mean Difference	Significance
1	2	2.00*	.004
	3	2.60*	.001
2	1	−2.00*	.004
	3	.60	.462
3	1	−2.60*	.001
	2	−.60	.462

$*p < 0.05.$

The Tukey HSD test reveals the most significant mean difference
between Class Size #1 and Class Size #3 (2.60), and at a very significant
alpha level of .001. No significant difference exists between Class Size #2
and Class Size #3 (.60) and at an unacceptable alpha level (.462). As with
the GB-STAT report, SPSS gives us evidence and reason to suspect that
something is happening between our smaller class size and larger class size.
Again, not cause and effect—but reason enough for further investigation
and study.

Conclusion

In our class size analysis, we found that a very significant difference existed between our small class size and large class size. Though the difference between the medium class size and the large class size was not so great, a pattern was revealed, leading us to suspect that students' acquisition of computer skills increased as class size was reduced. Perhaps this is not earth shattering, but think for a moment about how we generally use computers in our schools. My experience shows that most districts put their time, effort, and monies into the construction of big, fancy computer labs. We then fill them up with large classes.

As some districts are discovering, perhaps the better way to use computers is to dismantle the computer labs and distribute the computers out to the individual classrooms. Much evidence is surfacing to indicate that the optimum environment for computer instruction is three to five computers per classroom. As grand and impressive as computer labs are, they just may not be the best way to affect student achievement in computer skills or other areas of the curriculum.

I hope you see how the simple ANOVA can be used to help with the many decisions we must make regarding curriculum, student achievement, and assessment. The following examples at the end of this chapter are to assist you in using the ANOVA and understanding how we can use this statistical technique in our schools.

Application Activities

1. To test your comfort with the use of the F-distribution table for determining the critical F value, recall that an F ratio has two separate degrees of freedom (df): one for the numerator and one for the denominator. It is correct to report the numerator df first, followed by the denominator df. For example, if you are looking at (2, 12) as we did earlier, the 2 was read from the top of the table and the 12 from the left side. You will need both df values before consulting the F-distribution table. What can you determine if you see a report such as this: $F(2, 16) = 3.63$? How many treatment groups and how many students participated in this study?

2. As director of curriculum for your district, you are interested in piloting three different language arts programs. Your plan is to test their use in three different classes over the next semester. Set up a plan for conducting an analysis of variance for the three programs, with the goal of determining if either is more effective than the other or others.

7 Analysis of Variance

Repeated Measures

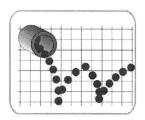

In Chapter 6, we learned how to use the ANOVA to test three groups (i.e., small, medium, and large class size). You recall that we used a computer assessment as the dependent variable (not manipulated). The independent variable (manipulated) was the class size. As you get more and more involved in using data analysis to improve your decision making in the schools, you begin to ask questions that involve other ways of using the ANOVA.

In our previous class size example, we set up our analysis with a single factor (one independent variable), which was the different class sizes. We also used an independent measures ANOVA because we used separate samples for each of the different class sizes. In Chapter 7, we will learn how to use the ANOVA for repeated measures—the same set of students analyzed in three different treatment situations. This technique is called *repeated measures analysis of variance.*

Let's Get Right to an Example

When I was working as a sixth-grade teacher for the Los Angeles Unified School District in the early 1980s, the Los Angeles Police Department implemented the now famous and nationally recognized D.A.R.E. program. As you know, the program's purpose is to educate students about the dangers of drugs, alcohol, tobacco, and gang violence.

As teachers, we were pretty convinced that students' attitudes toward drugs and alcohol changed for the better during their sixth-grade year when they were involved in the D.A.R.E. program. But our real question and concern was: Did students begin to revert back to their prior attitudes after the D.A.R.E. experience? In other words, could we determine whether the positive effects of the program were short or long term? Did students tend to revert back to their negative attitudes as they moved up into the junior high grades?

We administered a student attitudinal survey to a fifth-grade class to get an idea of their attitudes before D.A.R.E. involvement. We administered a similar attitudinal survey to the same class at the end of their sixth-grade year, after they completed the D.A.R.E. program. Finally, we administered the attitudinal survey to the same students after their completion of seventh-grade—1 full year after receiving the D.A.R.E. training. Table 7.1 displays a set of data representing the class studied along with their three separate attitudinal survey results.

The attitudinal survey consisted of 20 questions and statements that students responded to by answering on a Likert scale format (e.g., with options ranging from 1 = *strongly disagree* to 4 = *strongly agree*). Ten of the items were phrased positively and 10 phrased negatively, avoiding the tendency for respondents to agree with positive statements regardless of their content. The range of possible scores was 20 (for all 1's) to 80 (for all 4's). The higher score corresponded to a more positive attitude toward drugs, alcohol, and gangs. A sample statement follows:

	1	2	3	4
I believe smoking is always wrong.	Strongly Disagree	Disagree	Agree	Strongly Agree

For the fun of it, let's state the null and alternative hypotheses.

Null Hypothesis: There are no mean differences between the three different student groups' scores.

Alternative Hypothesis: There are mean differences between the three different groups' attitudinal scores.

TABLE 7.1 D.A.R.E. Attitudinal Survey Results

Student	5th Grade	6th Grade	7th Grade
1	54	62	56
2	57	62	52
3	44	56	45
4	46	58	48
5	55	60	58
6	54	65	56
7	57	62	52
8	44	58	45
9	46	60	48
10	55	62	58
11	54	65	56
12	57	62	52
13	44	54	45
14	46	55	48
15	55	62	52
16	54	65	56
17	57	62	52
18	44	58	45
19	46	60	48
20	55	62	58
21	54	65	56
22	57	62	52
23	44	50	45
24	46	58	48
25	55	62	58

The purpose of the ANOVA is to use the student sample data to determine which of the two hypotheses is more likely to be correct. In addition, we are interested to know whether, if there is a difference, it is statistically significant or just possibly due to chance. Let's review the four steps for hypothesis testing:

1. State the hypotheses and select an alpha level.

2. Decide on the degrees of freedom (*df*), and locate the critical region from the *F*-distribution table in Resource B.

3. Compute the test statistic.

4. Make a decision regarding the hypotheses.

Step 1

We have already stated our null and alternative hypotheses. Let's select the common alpha level of 05.

Step 2

Remember, with the ANOVA, we have two different degrees of freedom: one *df* between groups and another *df* between error. Hang on! This may sound a little complicated, but bear with me. Calculating the *df* between groups is no different than before ($N - 1$) or (3 groups – 1 group) = 2 *df*). Figuring the *df* between error is a bit more complex. We have 25 students ($25 - 1$), but we are assessing that group three times. So we must calculate ($25 - 1$) three times and add the results together ($24 + 24 + 24 = 72$), representing error between groups. We now subtract the *df* from within one group from the *df* between groups.

$$df \text{ error} = (75 - 3) - (25 - 1) = (72 - 24) = 48$$

For this analysis, the *df* equals (2, 48). Consulting the *F*-distribution table in Resource B, we find that the critical region required to reject the null hypothesis begins with $F = 3.19$. Remember, this means that the observed *F* value resulting from our ANOVA test must be 3.19 or greater for us to legitimately reject the null hypothesis of no difference between means of the three separate attitudinal assessments of our students at the alpha level of .05.

TABLE 7.2 ANOVA Summary Table for D.A.R.E. Attitudinal Survey and Grade Level

Source	Sum of Squares	df	Mean Square	F Ratio	Probability
Between subjects	1,354.34	24	56.43		
Within subjects	1,524	50			
Between groups	1,289.30	2	644.65	131.84	0.0001

Step 3 (GB-STAT)

Using GB-STAT (or SPSS), create a file titled "DARE ANOVA" using the data found in Table 7.1. Select **Statistics,** then **Analysis of Variance.** Highlight (bullet) **Repeated Measures, Multiple Columns as Cells,** and **One-Way Design.** You must then click on the button **Select Columns** on the right bottom of the screen. This is necessary to tell GB-STAT what columns we want to include in the ANOVA. As before, simply move "5th Grade," "6th Grade," and "7th Grade" to the selected samples box on the right side. Select **Done,** and the ANOVA summary table appears as shown in Table 7.2.

Step 4

To make a decision, the information we want is the F ratio and the probability (alpha level). The observed F ratio of 131.84 shown in the summary table is well beyond the required 3.19. Wow! The observed F ratio is 131.84—statistically significant and different enough for us to reject the null hypothesis of no difference. We accept our alternative hypothesis that there is a significant difference between the attitude assessments of our fifth-, sixth-, and seventh-grade students. And the significance level (alpha) is much lower than our selected .05, giving us more support for our position that this result did not just happen by chance.

TABLE 7.3 GB-STAT Tukey/Kramer Procedure for D.A.R.E. Attitudinal
Survey and Grade Level

	5th Grade	6th Grade	7th Grade
5th grade	0	210.77**	0.92
6th grade	210.77**	0	183.84**
7th grade	0.92	183.84**	0

$**p < 0.01.$

One More Question:
Where Does the Difference Lie?

Recall that the ANOVA tells us only that there is a difference. We want
to know if the difference is between fifth and sixth grades, between sixth
and seventh grades, or between fifth and seventh grades. Remember the
post hoc tests? We will seek help from the Tukey/Kramer procedure in iden-
tifying the exact location of the significant difference between means in our
three groups.

Go back to GB-STAT for a moment. From your ANOVA Summary
Table screen, select **Done,** which takes you back to the Analysis of Variance
screen. Select **Tukey/Kramer** from the **Multiple Comparisons** options, and
then double-click on **Tukey/Kramer.** The screen shown in Table 7.3
appears.

Before we analyze the Tukey/Kramer difference, you might also want to
print a visual display by clicking on the chart icon on the left upper part of
your GB-STAT screen. Figure 7.1 displays the result.

Tukey/Kramer Procedure

Without getting too technical, the Tukey HSD test measures the difference between the individual groups being compared in the ANOVA. As you
see in Table 7.3, the difference between the fifth-grade scores and the sixth-
grade scores is very significant at the .01 alpha level. Looking closely, we

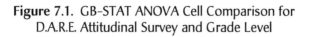

Figure 7.1. GB-STAT ANOVA Cell Comparison for
D.A.R.E. Attitudinal Survey and Grade Level

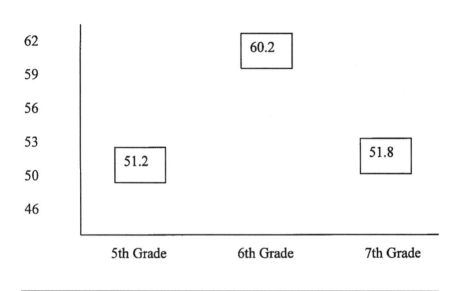

notice that the difference between the fifth-grade scores and the seventh-grade scores is not that great or significant, implying that the seventh-grade responses were somewhat similar to those in fifth grade. Why do you think there is such a significant difference between sixth- and seventh-grade responses? And is the difference in the same direction? Let's look at the cell comparison in Figure 7.1 for some help with these questions.

ANOVA Cell Comparison

In Figure 7.1, we see that the mean scores rise noticeably from the fifth grade to the sixth grade (51 to 60) but return to approximately the same mean in seventh grade. In other words, the positive attitudes increase during the time of the D.A.R.E. activities, but after a year later in seventh grade the attitudes seem to return to the level existing before the D.A.R.E. training (52).

Conclusion

We need to be careful that we do not create a *cause-and-effect* interpretation here. Some might argue that D.A.R.E. causes negative attitudes regarding drugs and alcohol because the attitudes declined after the first year. No, not necessarily! Perhaps the results are due to other societal factors (junior high school environment, the transition from elementary to junior high, etc.) that cause this change in attitudes. However, we are faced with the potential for some constructive data-driven decision making.

The finding does not indicate that the D.A.R.E. program is ineffective, but it may indicate to us that the efforts must continue for more than 1 year. In many large urban districts, the D.A.R.E. program is expanding into the seventh and eighth grades. Perhaps this is the reason. In addition, we as educators may want to look closely at our own curriculum and efforts. Perhaps there are some changes that we can make to curb undesirable attitudes about drugs and alcohol at the junior and senior high school levels.

For those of you who are not familiar with the D.A.R.E. program, the contact time with the D.A.R.E. officer consists of 1 or 2 hours a week. I might suspect that this short amount of time might produce short-term attitudinal effects and also that more contact hours per week might affect attitudes over a longer time. So you see, the "culprit" may not be the D.A.R.E. program itself but the extremely limited amount of time spent on activities and instruction. It is the data analysis that provides us with information helpful to the solution of the problem.

Application Activity

1. The dean and board of education of the newly opened charter school in the district are interested to see if reading comprehension increases significantly over the course of the year in third grade. The state department of education administers a reading indicator assessment three times per year that measures three levels of reading comprehension: (a) above average = 1, (b) average = 2, and (c) below average = 3.

In other words, the charter school administration would like to know if there are statistically significant changes in reading comprehension across the three assessments. The following data represent a sample of 10 third-grade students from the school:

Student	1st Assessment	2nd Assessment	3rd Assessment
1	1	1	1
2	3	3	2
3	2	2	1
4	2	2	2
5	2	1	1
6	3	3	2
7	1	1	1
8	2	1	1
9	3	2	2
10	1	1	2

a. Compute the mean score for each assessment.

b. Use a repeated measures ANOVA to determine if there are significant differences among the three assessment periods. Use the .05 level of significance.

8 Two-Way Analysis of Variance

Two Independent Variables

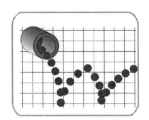

You're probably wondering! First he said that the Z-score method could be used to test hypotheses, then he said the *t* statistic was better. As soon as we thought the end was in sight, he presented the *independent-samples ANOVA* and continued with the *repeated-measures ANOVA*. We thought we were near the end—now what is this thing called *two-way analysis of variance*?

First of all, I assure you that this is the last chapter dealing with analysis of variance. Let me also assure you that if you feel pretty comfortable with the independent-measures ANOVA (Chapter 6), you will breeze through this chapter on the two-way ANOVA. So let's get on with it! What's the difference?

The basic strategies used in the one-way ANOVA apply as well to the two-way ANOVA. The statistic calculated in both is the *F* ratio. The *F* ratio serves the same purpose in the two-way ANOVA as it did in the one-way ANOVA: It helps us determine if the difference between means is different enough to be considered statistically significant or if it could have occurred by chance.

Our discussion and examples up to this point have focused on studies that have one independent variable (e.g., class size) and one dependent variable (e.g., a test or assessment). But in our school buildings and communities, variables rarely exist in such neat fashion. More often, many different variables are interacting simultaneously. We already suspect that the D.A.R.E. variable is not alone in influencing student attitudes. It is likely

TABLE 8.1 Two-Way ANOVA Matrix, Instructional Strategy by Content Area

	Math	*Reading*	*Science*
Cooperative learning	Scores for 20 students in math with cooperative learning	Scores for 20 students in reading with cooperative learning	Scores for 20 students in science with cooperative learning
Direct instruction	Scores for 20 students in math with direct instruction	Scores for 20 students in reading with direct instruction	Scores for 20 students in science with direct instruction

that other factors such as family life, school environment, and even gender take part in the creation of negative or positive attitudes toward drugs and alcohol.

The two-way ANOVA allows us to look at the effects and interactions of *two independent variables.* For example, we want to study student achievement in both cooperative learning and direct instruction situations. But we also want to look at different courses using each of the two instructional strategies. Table 8.1 displays the structure of a study examining the instructional delivery versus class content areas.

The first thing you probably notice is that the study involves separate samples of students rather than the same sample repeated. There are six different samples being tested, to be specific. Each cell in Table 8.1 contains a separate sample of students tested with the same dependent variable (standardized test). The two-way ANOVA will allow us to test for mean differences between the six instructional situations.

You can guess what our questions might be. Is there any difference in the two instructional strategies? Does perhaps one strategy work better in math whereas another works better in science? We might find evidence to support the use of cooperative learning as an effective teaching strategy in all three content areas (main effect). If this were the case, there would be no interaction between the two instructional strategies. Let's suppose, how-

Figure 8.1.
Main Effect Due to Type of Instructional Strategy

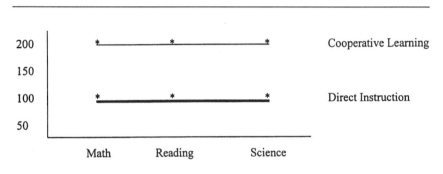

ever, that we find that cooperative learning reveals higher student achievement in math and reading but that direct instruction reveals higher student achievement in science (interaction). Figure 8.1 shows *main effect* due to the type of instructional strategy.

Figure 8.1 suggests that the two instructional strategies differ consistently in student achievement. The subject taught has no effect on student achievement with regard to the method of instruction. Slipping into statistical language for a moment, we observe a *main effect* due to the instructional strategy used in the classroom. We observe no *main effect* due to the content taught. We observe no *interaction* between instructional strategy used and content taught.

Figure 8.2 displays a different result. Often, the independent variables overlap or interact.

The data now reveal that cooperative learning seems to work well in math and science but perhaps not so well in reading. As you see, direct instruction appears to work best in reading but not so well in math and science. Interaction is occurring between instructional strategies and course content. Some combinations of instructional strategy and course taught result in higher student achievement than do other combinations. In Figure 8.2, we observe an *interaction* between instructional strategy and course taught.

As you now see, the two-way ANOVA allows you to evaluate the *main effect* of each factor individually and also the amount of *interaction* between

Figure 8.2. Interaction Between
Instructional Strategy and Content Taught

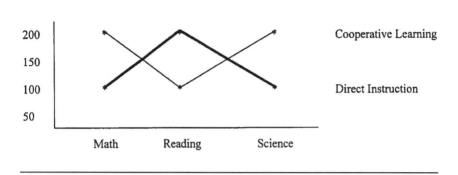

the two factors. Figure 8.2 shows only one possible example of interaction. You can readily see that a wide variety of results can occur.

Steps for the Two-Way ANOVA

The steps used in the two-way ANOVA are identical to the four steps we have been using all along for hypothesis testing.

1. State the null and alternative hypotheses, and set an alpha level.

2. Locate the critical region required to reject the null.

3. Compute the F ratios.

4. Make a decision regarding the hypotheses.

We will stay with our cooperative learning and direct instruction sample and work through a two-way ANOVA. The two-way ANOVA evaluates three separate hypotheses. Assuming that you can now create an alternative hypothesis from the null, let's just list the three null hypotheses.

1. There is no difference in student achievement between math, reading, and science classes.

TABLE 8.2 GB-STAT Test Data for Instructional Strategy and Content
Area

Students	Math/ Coop. Inst.	Math/ Direct Inst.	Reading/ Coop Inst.	Reading/ Direct Inst.	Science/ Coop Inst.	Science/ Direct Inst.
1	260	220	220	265	260	220
2	248	230	225	250	245	230
3	250	235	235	255	255	230
4	255	225	230	246	250	240
5	245	240	240	250	255	220

2. There is no difference in student achievement when students are taught with cooperative learning or direct instruction strategies.

3. The effect of instructional strategy does not depend on the course content (e.g., math, reading, or science).

The alternative hypotheses would state that there is a difference in student achievement between math, reading, and science classes; that there is a difference between classes taught by cooperative learning and classes taught by direct instruction strategies; and that there is interaction between instructional strategy and course content.

Table 8.2 displays six samples of students (five students in each) drawn from six different teaching situations: (a) math class/cooperative learning, (b) math class/direct instruction, (c) reading class/cooperative learning, (d) reading class/ direct instruction, (e) science class/cooperative learning, and (f) science class/direct instruction.

Using the data from Table 8.2, create a file titled "Coop/Direct Two-Way ANOVA." You may choose either to follow along with your computer or to go to GB-STAT after our discussion. Table 8.3 displays mean scores of the six different content area/instructional strategy combinations, as reported by GB-STAT.

It appears that scores are lowest in three learning situations: (a) direct instruction in math, (b) cooperative learning in reading, and (c) direct

TABLE 8.3 Mean Scores for the Content Area/Instructional Strategy Combinations

	Math	*Reading*	*Science*
Coop inst.	251.6	230	253
Direct inst.	230	253.2	228

instruction in science. Figure 8.3 displays this effect. Note that the mean scores decrease for cooperative learning in the reading class. For that same class (reading), the highest scores represent direct instruction as a more appropriate instructional strategy.

In addition to displaying sample descriptive statistics, GB-STAT produces an ANOVA summary table, as shown in Table 8.4. In our study, Factor A represents our three subject areas (math, reading, and science), and Factor B represents our two instructional strategies (cooperative learning and direct instruction).

From the table, we see that there is a statistically significant *main effect* for Factor B, Instructional Strategy, $F(2, 24) = 8.65$, $p < .05$. The table reports that there is not a statistically significant *main effect* for Factor A, Course Content, $F(2, 24) = .061$, $p > .05$. The *interaction* between the two factors is represented by A × B, which reveals a statistically significant interaction, $F(2, 24) = 34.29$, $p < .05$.

To *double-check* the accuracy of GB-STAT, let's look and see what the critical value is on the *F*-distribution table in Resource B. Remember that we have 2 and 24 different degrees of freedom (numerator and denominator). Reading our *F*-distribution table, we notice that for (2, 24), a critical value of 3.40 is required. In other words, there is significance if the observed value is 3.40 or greater at the .05 level of probability. The criteria is met with Factor B and A × B but not with Factor A.

Make a Decision About the Hypotheses

The results of our ANOVA test do not permit us to reject the first null hypothesis—that there is no difference in student achievement in math,

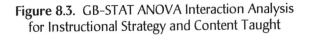

Figure 8.3. GB-STAT ANOVA Interaction Analysis
for Instructional Strategy and Content Taught

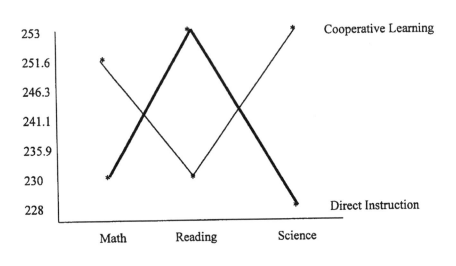

reading, and science. There was no statistically significant *main effect* for
Factor A. The results of our ANOVA test do permit us to reject the second
null hypothesis—that there is no difference between cooperative learning
and direct instruction as instructional strategies. The *main effect* for Factor
B was statistically significant. The results of our ANOVA test do permit us
to reject the third null hypothesis—that there is no interaction between
instructional strategies and class subjects. The ANOVA revealed a significant interaction between Factor A and Factor B.

Conclusion

I hope you feel more comfortable now with the two-way ANOVA. As
you see, logistically the one-way and two-way ANOVAs are similar. Both use
the same calculations, and both use the *F* distribution to test null hypothe-

TABLE 8.4 GB–STAT ANOVA Summary Table for Content Area (Factor A) and Instructional Strategy (Factor B)

Source	Sum Squares	df	Mean Square	F Ratio	Probability
Factor A	6.46	2	3.23	0.0613	.9407
Factor B	456.3	1	456.3	8.6502	.0071
A × B	3,611.19	2	1,809.09	34.2957	.0001
Within cell	1,265.99	24	52.75		
Total	5,346.96	29			

ses. Hopefully, you now see not only the additional power of the two-way ANOVA but also the potential for more exciting and useful statistical analyses in our schools and communities.

In the ANOVA test for differences in instructional strategies and course content, we did set out to "prove a case" for cooperative learning or direct instruction as the better way to teach. However, as you see by our sample study, evidence surfaced that might indicate that each method has its own strengths and applicability but perhaps in different situations (e.g., cooperative learning for math and science; direct instruction for reading).

The ongoing debate over cooperative learning and direct instruction is not unlike the ongoing debate over whole language and phonics. The real strength of our ANOVA test is perhaps the evidence that the two instructional strategies interact more than we sometimes think. To suggest to our teachers that they ought to use one or the other exclusively is a mistake. I have seen from my experience, as perhaps you have from yours, that our schools (and state and federal departments of education) often use a decision-making process driven by a need to accept one method or strategy and reject the others. The examples abound: (a) either whole language or phonics, (b) either standardized tests or performance-based assessment, (c) either constructivism or back to basics, and (d) either ESL or English only. The list goes on and on, doesn't it?

Too often, we do not recognize the strengths of several strategies in combination rather than alone. Our ANOVA points to the value of using the instructional strategies of cooperative learning and direct instruction in combination. Collecting sound data and analyzing appropriately will assist us in our decision making as we educators are faced with an almost daily barrage of the latest problems.

It is no secret that our profession is under careful scrutiny by our national and state legislators, communities, and, yes, the universities. I cannot imagine a better time for us to consistently use data to improve decision making in our schools for the benefit of our students. Yes, it is time consuming and in some cases costly. But what's our choice?

Application Activity

1. You are the principal of a large K-8 school district in central California. Each year, the high school counselors come to your school and present a reading readiness lecture to all eighth graders for the purpose of placement in language arts courses in ninth grade at the high school. One week after the lecture, the students are tested on the material covered in the lecture. You are interested to see if students score any differently if they attend the lecture in the auditorium rather than in their individual classrooms. In addition, you are interested to see whether students score differently on the assessment instrument if they receive the test in the auditorium as opposed to the regular classroom. You arrange to have half of the eighth graders hear the lecture in the auditorium and the other half hear the lecture in their classroom. Of the students hearing the lecture in the auditorium, half are tested in the same auditorium while the other half are tested in a classroom. Similarly, one half of the students hearing the lecture in the classroom are tested in the same classroom while the other half are tested in the auditorium. You end up with four groups of students with the test scores as shown in the following table. The scores represent correct answers on the assessment instrument.

	Auditorium Testing	*Classroom Testing*
Auditorium lecture	10	7
	12	9
	14	5
	10	8
	11	7
Classroom lecture	5	12
	9	15
	8	12
	9	11
	9	10

Using a two-factor ANOVA, determine if the size of the lecture facility and/ or the size of the testing facility has a statistically significant effect on the eighth graders' performance.

9 Correlation

My GRE Score Is Not
Good Enough for Harvard?

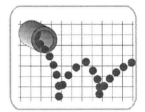

They told me that my GRE scores were not high enough to apply to Harvard (let me pretend for a moment). The Harvard admissions folks say that they take only freshmen with GRE scores of 1,200 and higher. Seems they have evidence that students with lower scores have a tendency to "not cut it" and to drop out at a higher rate than those with high GRE scores. They also have evidence that students with 1,200 and above have a tendency to do well at Harvard. Sound familiar?

Much of what we do as educators involves asking questions about two variables. Do students participating in extracurricular activities tend to perform better academically? Do boys tend to excel more than girls in math and computer applications (as we are led to believe), and/or do girls perform better in English and writing? Is there a relationship between GRE scores and success in college? All these questions involve a statistical technique called *correlation*. Quite simply, correlation is used to measure and describe a relationship between two variables.

Another Caution

There always seems to be a caution, huh? When finding correlation between two variables, we must guard against making the assumption that there is *cause and effect*. In other words, just because there is a strong corre-

Figure 9.1.
Relationship Between Drownings and Water Temperature

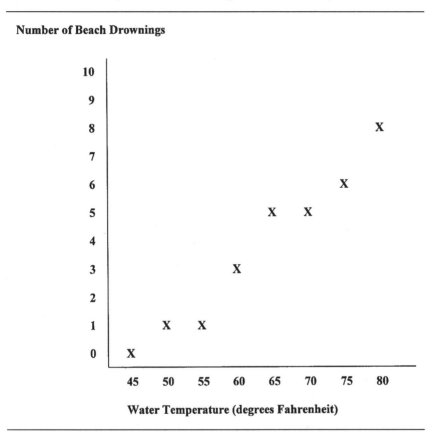

Number of Beach Drownings

Water Temperature (degrees Fahrenheit)

lation or relationship between X and Y, we cannot assume that X causes Y or Y causes X. Here's a rather simplistic but obvious example.

When studying the number of drownings on the beaches in California, researchers found a high correlation between water temperature and the number of drownings in the ocean. Figure 9.1 displays the correlation.

As the temperature of the ocean water increases, so does the number of drownings. This illustrates a *positive correlation*. As one variable increases, so does the other: maybe not in equal increments, but they both have a tendency to move in the same direction. In addition, as the temperature decreases, so does the number of drownings. The caution here is to guard against assuming that one variable *causes* the other. Here, it would be silly to assume that warm water *caused* drownings: There are obviously some other variables in play. Warm water means summer. Summer means more swimmers (and surfers) on the beaches and more swimmers in the water. A correlation may reveal that a relationship between two variables exists, but it does not report the reason why or suggest that one causes the other to occur.

When we discuss the extent to which two variables are related, we use a statistic called *Pearson correlation coefficient*. This coefficient (number) varies between –1.00 and +1.00. Both of these coefficients represent a perfect relationship between the variables, and 0.00 represents no correlation or the absence of a relationship. A *positive correlation* exists if students obtaining high scores on one variable tend to obtain high scores on a second variable or if students scoring low on one variable tend also to score low on a second variable.

Time Out for
Some Statistical Jargon

The technical name for the Pearson correlation is the *Pearson product-moment correlation coefficient*. Where did that name come from? In statistics, the deviations about the mean are called *moments,* and if you multiply two moments together, you get the *product* of moments. If you were a statistician named Karl Pearson and you created a way to measure the correlation between two variables, might you call the procedure the Pearson product-moment correlation? The statistical symbol is the letter r, so we shorten the name to *Pearson r.*

Back to Our Discussion

Colleges and universities require our graduating seniors to take either the SAT or the ACT because a positive correlation exists between high ACT or SAT scores and academic success at the university. You may ask, How positive? Well, certainly not a perfect +1.00 correlation. That would mean there were no exceptions and all successful college students had high GRE scores (and to the same degree). I, along with a few of you, probably would wish to question this correlation. In actuality, the correlation is approximately +.60, meaning the relationship is positive (direction) and pretty strong (strength). Simply, correlations only tell us two things: (a) the direction of the relationship (positive or negative) and (b) the strength of the relationship (0 to + or −1.00).

A negative (−) correlation exists if students who score low on one variable tend to score high on a second variable or if students scoring high on the first variable tend to score low on the second variable. A good example is the fact that sometimes students who score very high in math and science tend to score low in English and language arts. Here at the university, we struggle with the evidence that suggests a negative correlation between the ability of athletes and their grade point average such that as the athletic ability of athletes increases, their grade point average tends to decrease. Again, not a perfect negative correlation (−1.00), but strong enough to cause coaches and university presidents concern. The current solution, though not very successful, is to provide tutors for athletes. You can guess the problem with this solution. What about tutors for nonathletes? Do we offer them the same treatment? Most of the faculty and student body believe not.

I think it is helpful to repeat that correlation measures only two aspects of a relationship: (a) strength (reported by the decimal) and (b) direction (reported by the− or + sign). For instance, a correlation of +.95 means a very strong relationship (almost a perfect 1.00) in a positive direction. A correlation coefficient of −.95 means a very strong relationship (almost a perfect 1.00) in a negative direction. Figure 9.2 displays a series of scatter diagrams illustrating a variety of correlations (relationships) between two variables.

As you notice, the greater the tendency for the student scores to fall on a straight line, the closer to a perfect correlation (+1.00 or −1.00). If no pattern or linear relationship exists, the correlation approximates 0.00.

Why Would Educators Be
Interested in Correlations?

The main purpose of this book is to present statistical tools and applications useful to teachers, administrators, and central office personnel as they make decisions for school improvement. So get to it! Tell me how correlations will help me in my daily life as an educator.

Figure 9.2.
Correlations or Relationships Between Two Variables

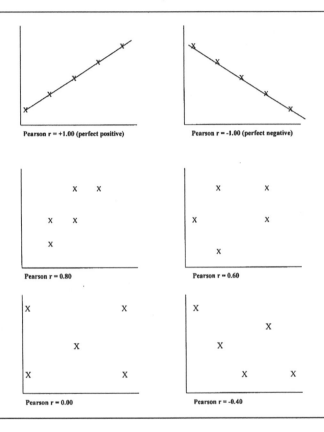

Let's return to the California beaches for a moment. We find a strong positive correlation (strength and direction) between warm water temperatures and the number of drownings. Realizing that this is not a causal relationship, we can perhaps *predict* the number of drownings to increase during the months of July and August, when water temperatures are highest. Therefore, we might decide to double the number of lifeguards on duty or position a number of lifeguards on surfboards to better guard against the potential for drowning. In this example, the correlation was used to *predict* and hopefully to reduce the number of drownings—data-driven decision making.

A Junior High School
Music Program

Bob, a junior high school music teacher, works in a district that makes a strong commitment to music and the arts in its curriculum. The community is as proud of its music program as it is of its athletic teams. It is not surprising that Bob is expected to have a first-class junior high school band and orchestra. The community and central office have a long tradition of support (both financial and otherwise) for their music program. Because Bob is also the music teacher in the two elementary schools feeding into the junior high school, he has the opportunity to train excellent elementary students in the beginning band and orchestra who will later move into his nationally recognized junior high school band and orchestra.

Bob's ongoing effort, and what keeps him awake some nights, is recruiting. How can he effectively recruit quality musicians for his junior high program? How can he *predict* that the students he selects at the elementary level will mature and develop into the excellent musicians required in his junior high school performing groups? His hunch or *hypothesis* is that there might be a relationship between students' academic performance and their performance or success in music. Though he realizes there are exceptions to this rule, he still believes there might be something to his hunch.

Bob decides to look at the relationship between students' success in music and their disaggregated Iowa Test of Basic Skills results. In other words, he suspects that there may be a relationship between certain academic areas (e.g., reading, math, science, social studies) and musical ability. Maybe students who are good readers learn to read music better and faster. Maybe students who work well in science lab groups together possess the collaborative skills necessary to perform musically with others.

He collects the final music grades from his last 4 years of junior high school music students, transforming letter grades to grade point equivalents. Table 9.1 displays his grade transformation strategy.

Bob then wants to see if a relationship exists between music performance grades and students' individual ITBS scores. The answers to his questions might help with his recruiting at the elementary level. He reasons that if a high number of students who perform at a high level in music also share a characteristic of high science scores, there will be a positive correlation between the two. If so, he will consider using science scores at the elementary level as a predictor of future success in his junior high school band

TABLE 9.1 Music Grade Transformation Scale

Grade	GPA
A+	4.5
A	4.0
A–/B+	3.5
B	3.0
B–/C+	2.5
C	2.0
C–	1.5
D/F	1.0

TABLE 9.2 Relationship Between Music Grades and ITBS Science Test Scores (Hypothetical)

Music Student	Music Grades	Science Scores
1	2.5	180
2	4.0	210
3	3.5	200
4	4.5	220
5	3.0	190

and orchestra. Table 9.2 displays a small sample of *hypothetical* data and how this correlation might look if Bob's hypothesis were correct.

First, you notice that there is a pattern of both variables moving in the same direction. The student with a music GPA of 2.5 scores 180 on the science assessment. The student with a music GPA of 3.0 scores 190 on the science assessment. Looking further at each of the higher GPAs, we see a corresponding increase in science scores. We know that the correlation is going to be positive (direction) because both variables are moving in the same increasing manner. Do we know how strong the relationship is? Not exactly—but let's look closer. Remember, a perfect correlation could exist if the increases were incremental and increased the same amount between each of the five GPAs. Sure enough, each increase of 0.5 in GPA equals a science score increase of 10 points. Can you guess what the correlation coefficient is in this example? Yes, a perfect correlation of +1.00. As one variable increases, the other variable increases by an equal amount. How likely is this to occur in real life? Not very. Though the example is not realistic, I hope it helped to conceptualize the correlation procedure. Now let's go back to Bob and his real-life dilemma.

GB-STAT and SPSS—Help!

Before we rush into correlations on the computer, allow me to digress for a moment. Yes, there is a formula for calculating correlation coefficients by hand. As has been the practice in this book, I will not emphasize or encourage the use of formulas for calculations. With your permission, however, allow me to touch on the issue lightly. As much as I encourage the early use of computer software for statistical analysis, there is a caution (here he goes again—another caution). Sometimes it is detrimental to rush into computer analysis, especially if you are having difficulty with the conceptual understanding of the procedure. In those cases, it can be helpful to calculate a small sample by hand to get the basic understanding of the process. As promised, I will not elaborate on complex formulas and calculations—the calculation of the Pearson notwithstanding. However, you might want to consult a formal statistics text and review the hand calculation of the Pearson *r,* using the *raw score method.* It is actually pretty straightforward, using nothing more than squaring, summing, cross products, and the square root.

Okay, enough of that. Using data from Resource C, create a file titled "Music Correlation." You will notice Bob's sample of 24 music students, their music grades, and their set of scores for math, language, and science. Remember Bob's question: Is there perhaps a correlation or relationship between students' music performance and their academic performance? And if so, can he use the information to help recruit and select music students at the elementary level for his junior high band and orchestra?

TABLE 9.3 GB-STAT Correlation Matrix for Band Grades and Academic
Test Scores

	Band Grades	Math Scores	Language Scores	Science Scores
Band grades	1.00	0.874**	0.0159	0.0848
Math scores	0.874**	1.00	0.1942	0.2441
Language scores	0.0159	0.1942	1.00	0.3105
Science scores	0.0848	0.2441	0.3105	1.00

**$p < 0.01$.

GB-STAT

After opening the "Music Correlation" file, select **Statistics** and then **Descriptive Statistics**. The pop-up menu asks for a check on **Simple Correlation** and a check on **Include All Variables**. Be certain that you see next to *Variables Selected* the number 4. If the number 4 is not there, you did not check the Include All Variables box. Another screen will appear asking you to select your variables. As before, add the four variables to the box on the right side of the screen. Selecting **Go** creates a correlation matrix with the four selected variables of (a) Band Grades, (b) Math Scores, (c) Language Scores, and (d) Science Scores. In this example, Bob is interested in calculating a Pearson product-moment correlation for each pair of variables. In addition, Bob is testing the null hypothesis that the correlation between music grades and academic grades equals zero. His alternative hypothesis is obviously that the correlation does not equal zero. The matrix is reproduced and displayed in Table 9.3.

You should first realize that correlation matrices display each correlation twice in the square matrix. Correlations of 1.00 are at points where each variable meets with itself. For example, Band Grades correlated with themselves (Band Grades) equals a perfect positive correlation of 1.00. The same is true of the other three variables. The upper right triangle of the matrix formed by the diagonal of 1.00's is a mirror image of the lower left triangle. As an example, please note the upper right cell of the matrix (Science: 0.0848). Now, note the lower left cell of the matrix (same information—Science: 0.0848).

Now let's see what the matrix reveals. Bob is interested in three pieces of information: (a) the relationship between music and math, .874 (b) the relationship between music and language, .0159 and (c) the relationship between music and science, 0.0848. First of all, the relationship (correlation) between music and language and music and science is positive, but very low and almost nonexistent. Remember, as the coefficient approximates zero, it reveals less and less relationship or correlation.

The matrix reveals a correlation of .874 between music grades and math. This correlation is positive and quite strong. As the coefficient approximates 1.00, it reveals more and more relationship between the variables. You also notice that GB-STAT (like SPSS) flags the statistically significant correlations. The music grades/math correlation is so strong (significant) that GB-STAT shows an alpha level (p) of .01. Our selected alpha level is usually only .05, but in this case the correlation meets the more stringent .01 level. To review, the result is considered statistically significant if the p value is less than the chosen alpha level. In Bob's analysis, the p value is much less than the selected .05, so he has reason to reject the null hypothesis of no difference between music grades and math scores. However, the null hypotheses of no difference between music grades and language and science scores must be accepted because their correlations are insignificant and less strong.

SPSS

After opening the "Music Correlation" file, select **Statistics** (in Version 8) or **Analyze** (in Version 9) from the menu bar. Select **Correlate,** then **Bivariate.** A box appears asking for a selection of variables. As in GB-STAT, highlight the four variables, and move them to the box on the right of the screen. Be sure you check *Pearson, Two-Tailed,* and **Flag significant correlations.** You will also notice the opportunity for **Options** if you wish to display descriptive statistics such as means and standard deviations. Select **OK,** and the Pearson r correlation matrix appears as shown in Table 9.4.

TABLE 9.4 SPSS Correlation Matrix for Band Grades and Academic Test
Scores

	Band Grades	Math Scores	Language Scores	Science Scores
Band grades				
Pearson r	1.000	.874**	.016	.085
Sig.		.000	.941	.694
N	24	24	24	24
Math scores				
Pearson r	.874**	1.000	.194	.244
Sig.	.000		.363	.250
N	24	24	24	24
Language scores				
Pearson r	.016	.194	1.000	.310
Sig.	.941	.363		.140
N	24	24	24	24
Science scores				
Pearson r	.085	.244	.310	1.000
Sig.	.694	.250	.140	
N	24	24	24	

**Correlation is significant at the 0.01 level (two-tailed).

So What Does This Mean for Bob?

Remembering the caution issued earlier to guard against assuming
cause and effect with correlations, we note that Bob's analysis does not
prove that students who receive high grades in math also develop into exem-
plary musicians. However, there is sufficient reason to believe that perhaps

for some reason (unknown at this point) there is a relationship between math and music achievement. We might conjecture that music possesses mathematical qualities (actually it does) and that students who are good in math may progress in music faster and with greater success. I assume Bob will look more closely at the relationship and probably will use this correlation result in his recruiting plans at the elementary level.

Other Data-Driven Decision Making

Though Bob was not interested in looking at the relationships of the other variables to each other, the analysis reveals something of interest for the rest of us. What were the correlations between the three subjects? Not so significant. In other words, students receiving high grades in math were not really achieving high grades in language and science. This is somewhat unusual, for we know from previous studies that in general high-achieving students in one subject area tend to also do well in others. Not a perfect correlation, but pretty strong and positive.

As Bob's building principal, I think I would want to investigate further or conduct further studies in an attempt to discover why those students' language and science scores were noticeably lower. However, Bob might argue (and with justification) that this finding just points to the relationship between performance in music and high achievement in mathematics. Again, the Pearson *r* correlation does not reveal reasons for the correlation, but there certainly is a reason for concern. I think my first step would be to talk with the teachers of the students in question to get another assessment of their performance in language and science. Perhaps their actual performance is different from the results of our standardized test. A couple other questions come to mind. Can we really assess language skills so easily on standardized tests? Can we really appropriately assess science skills on a standardized test? Maybe our assessment procedures in language and science should include more performance-based strategies.

A common result in statistical analysis: More questions have been raised than answered. However, this is not cause for despair but cause for celebration. We as educators need to harness some of the power and potential of data analysis with regard to decision making at the school site. I will have more to say about this issue in my concluding chapter.

The Spearman Correlation

Again, without getting too technical, I will touch lightly on the Spearman correlation, which is used in a different situation. The Spearman correlation measures the relationship between variables that are placed on an *ordinal scale* of measurement. Sometimes we have data that are in rank order. For instance, the cafeteria cooks are interested in students' preference for different menu items. Five meals are presented in a survey form, and students respond with answers of first, second, third, fourth, and fifth choice. If we were to conduct a correlational study with menu preference, we would use the Spearman method. You will notice that in both GB-STAT and SPSS there is an option for selecting this correlational strategy. We will not discuss the Spearman further because all of our example in this book deal with the Pearson *r*.

Conclusion

In my experience as a teacher, principal, superintendent, and now university professor, I think the majority of questions and concerns I have had over the years have really been correlational. Most questions and concerns related to teaching and learning involve the degree to which two variables go together. If we can identify the variable or variables that influence a certain behavior, there is a tremendous potential for helping students become successful. If there is only one statistical tool that I could pass on to you, it would be correlation. Let me close this chapter on correlation with a recent study conducted at an area school district.

Collaborative Teaching and Integrated Curriculum

I was approached by a school district superintendent a year ago. John was concerned about the lack of collaborative instructional activities at his high school. As is common in many high schools, often our curriculum is so compartmentalized that we create learning environments boxed in with four walls. This box is math, this other box is English, and this one over here is just for science. You know, you have been there. Teachers can become very territorial and specialized in such an environment.

John's desire was to help his faculty realize the interconnectedness of different subject areas. He was aware of much of the research that indicates that students can study math in a gymnasium. Language skills are also encouraged in science classes. The evidence goes on and on. John began by asking if we could look at his school's data in an effort to improve his wish for a more integrated curriculum at this high school.

In looking at the district standardized and performance-based assessment data, we discovered what John suspected—there was a very high correlation between the individual course assessment results and student achievement. The relationships between achievement in one course and achievement in others was pretty strong and positive. In other words, students who did well in English also had a tendency to do well in math, science, and other courses. This was not earth shattering to discover, but it caused John to begin thinking and asking the following questions:

> If I can show my faculty the strong correlation between student achievement across the various subject areas, might it help them realize the interconnectedness of all learning? Maybe we can talk about how our math teachers and English teachers can develop collaborative activities that would benefit both subject areas at the same time. Doesn't it make sense to blend science and math together when the two courses use so many similar skills?

John's plan moved forward. His objective progressed to the point that his faculty began to agree that perhaps this thing called *correlation* had some benefit as they struggled with ways to improve their curriculum and develop a more collaborative teaching and learning environment at the high school.

As always seems to happen, data analysis poses more questions to ponder. In the process of looking at correlations, the faculty even noticed some significant findings related to gender. They were encouraged to find out that there was no significant correlation between math achievement and gender. In other words, girls were achieving just as consistently as boys in math and were equally represented in the advanced math classes such as trigonometry and calculus.

However, one finding surfaced that concerned both the administration and staff. There seemed to be a significant correlation between English composition assessment and gender. A great number of the girls were receiving the higher grades, and in general boys were not performing as well. Again, maybe this is not an earth-shattering finding, but this particular group of faculty and administration decided they would not be satisfied with this result.

At the end of a particular workshop with the faculty, I was approached by the high school principal. He reluctantly offered his solution to the problem of composition and gender, stating that he did not feel comfortable offering his remarks to the entire faculty. His theory (or hypothesis) was that for years all the high school composition teachers had been female and had had a tendency to assign topics for writing that were of more interest to girls than boys. He was not meaning to appear "sexist" with his comments; rather, he was suggesting that there might be a correlation between assigned topics in composition and student achievement.

The end of this story is a happy one. The principal eventually presented his hypothesis to his three English composition faculty, and, to his surprise, they agreed that perhaps the assignments in the class needed to be reviewed. Again, proof? No, but a pattern uncovered by a correlation study that presented the opportunity for some real data-driven decision making. The result was two decisions: (a) More thought would go into the choice of composition assignments, offering a wider variety of topic choices, and (2) the composition and science faculty developed and implemented several collaborative activities that had students using writing skills in science but also encouraged students to suggest science-related topics in composition class.

Application Activities

1. Create a data file using the math and language scores for a small group of students at your school. Conduct a Pearson correlation between student math and language test scores. The question is: What is the relationship between mathematical skill and verbal skill? What does the test reveal, and what might be some of the instructional reasons for the outcome for this particular group of students?

2. Select 20 students from your school. Create a GB-STAT or SPSS data file that includes the students' standardized test scores for science and math. One of your questions is: Do students who receive high test scores in math also have a tendency to receive high test scores in science? Disaggregate the data by breaking them down into two groups, male and female. When you run separate correlations on males and females, are there noticeable patterns of differences in strength and direction of correlation coefficients?

10 Putting It All Together

*A Data-Driven
Practice Field*

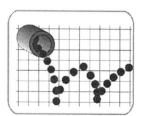

Earlier, I emphasized that educators rarely examine the data existing in schools to assess in a systematic way the quality of teaching and learning in our schools. Much if not all of the fault lies with the universities and their failure to adequately prepare teachers and administrators to deal with data. I agree totally with Holcomb's (1999) contention that existing programs at the university level (and the course delivery of statistics and tests and measurement classes) have created a structure that emphasizes esoteric experimental designs that cannot be replicated in a normal school setting. I also echo Bracey's (1997) belief that in all too many instances we teach statistics and other data-related courses in a theoretical manner based on hard-to-understand formulas and far too few examples related to the daily life of education practitioners. It is my belief that herein lies the problem.

Practice and Performance Fields

For some time, I have studied the work of Daniel Kim, an organizational consultant and public speaker who is committed to helping problem-solving organizations transform into learning organizations. Kim is a colleague of Peter Senge (*The Fifth Discipline,* 1990) and cofounder of the MIT Organizational Learning Center, where he is currently the director of the Learning Lab Research Project.

Kim (1995) argued that the accelerated pace of change has overwhelmed our ability to keep up with and understand how these changes affect our organization. We lack a place to practice decision making where we can make mistakes and step out of the system temporarily so that we can work "on" it and not just "in" it. He calls such a place "a managerial practice field."

Think for a moment about our jobs in education. Except for a brief experience with some sort of internship or student teaching (both of which continue to suffer from a lack of quality and relevance), where and when do we get an opportunity to leave the day-to-day pressures temporarily and enter a different kind of space in which we can practice and learn? Think for another moment about your limited training and preparation in the use of data in effective decision making. What has been missing? The opportunity or place did not exist where aspiring teachers or administrators could improve their skills in problem analysis, program and student evaluation, data-based decision making, and report preparation. In addition, if a practice field did exist, it did not emphasize the relevance of statistics and data analysis to the day-to-day lives of teachers and administrators. Let me return to the work of Daniel Kim for just a moment.

Imagine you are walking across a tightrope stretched between the World Trade Towers in New York City. The wind is blowing and the rope is shaking as you inch your way forward. One of your teammates sits in the wheelbarrow you are balancing in front of you, while another perches on your shoulders. There are no safety nets, no harnesses. You think to yourself, "One false move and the three of us will be taking an express elevator straight down to the street." Suddenly your trainer yells from the other side, "Try a new move! Experiment! Take some risks! Remember, you are a learning team!" (p. 353)

Kim argued that though this may sound ludicrous, it is precisely what many companies expect their management teams to do—experiment and learn in an environment that is risky, turbulent, and unpredictable. Unlike a high-wire act or sports team, however, management teams do not have a practice field in which to learn; they are nearly always on the performance field.

Replace the words *management teams* with *teachers* or
in the passage above. Will you not agree that our jobs in educa
the high-wire act described by Kim?

A Data-Driven Practice Field

It is my desire in this final chapter to provide you with a "practice field"
designed around the actual work we do in schools. This practice field will
also give you the opportunity to practice each of the data analysis strategies
discussed in earlier chapters. In addition, you will have the opportunity to
experiment with alternative strategies, test some of your assumptions, and
practice working with the data found in your schools.

One of the goals of this chapter is to provide a *real enough* practice field
so that the activities are meaningful to you as an educator but also *safe
enough* to encourage experimentation and learning. Hopefully, you will be
able to step out of the day-to-day pressures faced in your workplace and
spend time in this practice field. World-class athletes practice. Musicians
practice. But educators for the most part, are constantly performing.

Again, part of the cause is teacher and administrator preparation programs. Because I am more familiar with and involved in administrative
preparation, allow me to make a few comments. Murphy and Forsyth
(1999) reported that although supervised practice could be the most critical
phase of the administrator's preparation, the component is notoriously
weak. Along with other education leaders (Griffiths, 1998; Milstein, 1990),
Murphy claimed that field-based practices do not involve an adequate number of experiences and are arranged on the basis of convenience.

I am fully aware of the difficulties encountered when attempting to provide aspiring administrators with rich and relevant practice in the real-life
setting of the school. The most difficult task is trying to provide these experiences while the aspiring administrator continues with his or her full-time
teaching position. I believe the most practical and logical solution to this
dilemma requires preparation programs to step forward and provide this
practice field in place of some of the excessive theoretical and traditional
program content at the university.

TABLE 10.1 Horizon High School: Coding of Variables

Gender:	Gender of the student: 1 = male, 2 = female
Ethnic:	Ethnicity of the student: 1 = white, 2 = Hispanic, 3 = black
Freeredu:	Qualification for free/reduced lunch: 1 = yes, 2 = no
Math:	Standardized test scores in math
Language:	Standardized test scores in language
Science:	Standardized test scores in science
Writing:	District-created writing assessment scores
Grade:	Present grade level of student
GPA:	Current grade point average of student

I also believe that many of our individual courses (e.g., in applied educational statistics) should have a practice field where educators can apply what they learn away from the pressures of day-to-day school business and experiment with new ideas and assumptions. What follows is an attempt to place you in such a practice field.

Horizon High School

Using the data found in Resource D, create a file titled "Horizon High School Data." The data represent 100 students in grades 9 through 12. Though the data are fictitious, the variables and entries represent the same kind of data found in your school. Table 10.1 displays the variables and coding used.

Activity 1: Frequency Distributions and Cross-Tabulation

With the use of frequency distributions and cross-tabulations in GB-STAT or SPSS, we would like to take a quick glimpse of the Horizon High School student body. For example, we want to know:

1. The number of males and females

2. The ethnic makeup of the school

3. The number of students qualifying for free/reduced lunch

4. The number of students in each grade

Though you may not consider the number of males and females or the ethnic makeup of the school as terribly important, the information regarding ethnicity and free/reduced lunches is used for most of your funding formulas, grant applications, and state and federal reimbursements.

You might also want to obtain a graphic representation of your frequency distributions for Horizon High School. Simply select **Chart,** and then select the desired graphic form, such as **Bar Chart.** Be certain to select the graphic choice after you select your variables but before you select **OK** or **GO** to run your frequency distribution.

Questions

1. Is there anything unusual about the number of boys qualifying for free/reduced lunch compared to the number of girls? For what reason might this information be relevant?

2. Does the gender representation seem normal for an average high school? Is there any weighted effect between gender and any of the other variables?

Discussion

Tables 10.2, 10.3, and 10.4 display some of the information that we need to address the questions above.

Examining data by the use of frequency distributions and tabulation tables allows us to determine very quickly and easily what our population or sample looks like. Such information as gender, age, race, and socioeconomic status is helpful before we proceed with further investigation.

TABLE 10.2 Gender of Horizon High School Students

	No.	%	Cumulative %
Male	53	53	53
Female	47	47	100
Total	100	100	

TABLE 10.3 Gender of Horizon High School Students by Free/Reduced Lunch Qualification

	Free/Reduced Lunch		
Gender	Yes	No	Total
Male	13	40	53
Female	19	28	47
Total	32	68	100

TABLE 10.4 Ethnicity of Horizon High School Students

Ethnicity	No.	%	Cumulative %
White	56	56	56
Hispanic	28	28	84
Black	16	16	100
Total	100	100	

Activity 2: Measures of Central Tendency and Variability

You serve as the chairperson of the Horizon High School Curriculum Committee. The director of secondary education in your district has just notified you that she wants a recommendation from you and the committee

TABLE 10.5 Horizon Students' Test Score Data Descriptive Statistics

Subject	N	Minimum	Maximum	Mean	SD
Math	100	234	263	246.86	7.69
Language	100	232	260	248.26	6.38
Science	100	220	276	245.41	8.51
Writing	100	175	234	205.76	11.88

for this year's textbook adoption. As is the practice at Horizon High School, the board of education allows only one subject area to have new textbooks annually. You and your committee must decide which subject area will receive this year's new textbooks.

Looking at the standardized test scores for Horizon High School, can you use the measures of central tendency and variability to help you and your committee make a wise decision and recommendation to the director of secondary education?

Questions

1. Based on the standardized test data you have for Horizon High School, which subject area might you and your committee recommend for new textbooks this year? And what reasons would you give for your decision?

2. The mean and standard deviation of which subject area might concern you? Approximately 68% of your students scored between what two points in that same subject area? Does it perhaps make sense that the standard deviation in this subject area might be higher than in other subject areas? Why or why not?

Discussion

Table 10.5 displays some of the information we need to address the questions above.

We do notice that the mean scores for the writing assessments are much lower (on average) than those for other subject areas. In addition, the standard deviation is higher than the others, meaning that the writing scores are a bit more spread out from the mean. Specifically, we can say that approximately 68% of the high school students scored between 194 and 218 on their writing assessment scores. The standard deviation is 11.88 (rounded to 12), and the mean is 205.76 (rounded to 206). The 12 points represent one standard deviation unit, and we know that approximately 68% of a distribution falls between one standard deviation unit below the mean and one standard deviation unit above the mean.

The scores of the other subject areas are noticeably higher and the standard deviations a bit smaller, indicating that those scores are centered a little more closely on the mean. Though we need to take many other factors into consideration, the writing scores give us reason to perhaps suggest new instructional materials for that subject area.

Activity 3: A One-Sample t Test

The national testing service responsible for the publishing of your standardized tests states that the average score across the nation on the math assessment is 240. Your principal has asked that you prepare a report to the Horizon Board of Education and wants you to specifically address the progress of your high school students in mathematics. Can you use a one-sample t test to help you with your report?

Remember, a one-sample t test is a procedure used to determine if the mean of a distribution differs significantly from a preset value. In other words, does the mean of the Horizon High School math scores differ significantly from the preset value of 240, which represents the national average? As an appropriate test of significance, the one-sample t test compares a sample mean with a single fixed value.

Questions

1. Are the Horizon High School students' scores significantly different (higher or lower) from the national average as measured by the standardized math assessment you currently use?

2. Using the same national average score of 240, what can you say about your high school students in the other subject areas?

TABLE 10.6 SPSS One–Sample *t* Test for Math Scores

		One-Sample Statistics		
	N	*Mean*	*SD*	*Std. Error Mean*
Math	100	246.86	7.69	.77

		One-Sample Test (Test Value = 240)		
	t	*df*	*Sig.*	*Mean Diff.*
Math	8.923	99	.000	6.86

Discussion

Table 10.6 displays information helpful in addressing the Horizon School Board regarding the math achievement of your high school students.

Good news for you and the board of education. This one-sample *t* test indicates that the mean score of your high school students in math (246.86) is significantly higher than the national average of 240. With a significance level of .05 and 99 degrees of freedom, the *t* value required for significance is approximately 1.9, as shown in Resource A. You notice from your test report that the *t* value of 8.923, with a significance level much lower than your selected .05 (.000), is well into the critical region required to reject the null hypothesis of no significant difference between your high school students and the national average. Recall that SPSS rounds to three decimal places, so the significance level is probably around .0004.

Using a one-sample *t* test to compare the national average of 240 with the other subject areas reveals that both science and language means are also significantly higher than the national average. However, you will notice that the one-sample *t* test for writing reveals that the mean score is significantly *lower* than the national average, as shown in Table 10.7.

This draws attention to why we want to conduct a two-tailed test. We are interested in any difference—higher or lower. In this case, the significance is equally important to know. The board of education will no doubt

TABLE 10.7 SPSS One-Sample *t* Test for Writing Scores

	One-Sample Statistics			
	N	*Mean*	*Std. Deviation*	*Std. Error Mean*
Writing	100	205.76	11.88	1.19

	One-Sample Test (Test Value = 240)			
	t	*df*	*Sig.*	*Mean Diff.*
Writing	−28.811	99	.000	−34.24

feel pretty good about what is happening in math, science, and language but will have some concerns about the writing scores. Certainly you have some ideas about what kinds of data-driven decision making might be appropriate in this case.

Activity 4: An Independent-Samples t Test

You have taught high school algebra, geometry, and trigonometry for over 10 years at Horizon High School. Though your superintendent has tried to recruit a woman or two for the math department, the department continues to be dominated by male instructors. With the increased attention and emphasis on Title IX and gender equity in the media and on our campuses, educators must be aware and remain sensitive to the issues of gender equity in both academic and extracurricular activities.

A local parent activist group has approached your school board and made the claim that because of the male dominance of math instructors, they suspect that male students are receiving better instruction and more attention in math subjects than the female students. Specifically, they claim that boys are outperforming girls in math achievement.

Your superintendent has asked you to report your assessment of the situation at the Friday afternoon faculty meeting. Use an independent-samples

TABLE 10.8 Independent-Samples Test: Gender and Math Scores

	Group Statistics			
	N	*Mean*	*SD*	*Std. Error Mean*
Math				
Male	53	245.36	7.83	1.08
Female	47	248.55	7.24	1.06

	Independent-Samples Test			
	t Test for Equality of Means			
	t	*df*	*Sig.*	*Mean Diff.*
Math (equal variances assumed)	−2.110	98	.037	−3.19

t test with a significance level of .05 to help prepare for your faculty presentation on Friday.

Questions

1. Do the males and females differ significantly from each other on standardized math test performance?

2. What unusual finding presents itself, and how might you explain this finding to the faculty and superintendent on Friday?

3. How might you use data-driven decision making to address the gender issue in mathematics at Horizon High School?

Discussion

As displayed in Table 10.8, we find there is a 3.19 difference between the means (male = 245.36; female = 248.55). Obviously, we discover that the girls are actually outperforming the boys in standardized math scores. Again, the real question is: Is the difference great enough to be statistically significant? This finding will hopefully appease the parent group, but we still have a problem, don't we? It was our belief that boys and girls were performing equally. Does this *prove* that we are delivering instruction unfairly or inequitably? Not necessarily, but it reveals a pattern and a concern.

Looking closely at our *t*-test report, we find a statistically significant difference between our girls' and boys' math performance. The *t* value of –2.110 is beyond the 1.9 required for null hypothesis rejection. Note that the *t* value is negative, indicating that the mean score for boys is significantly lower than the mean score for the girls. Again, the reason for two-tailed tests—we are equally concerned with negative significance.

What kinds of instructional decisions might your department and faculty make to address the gender issue discovered? Are other variables perhaps in play here? Is this definitely a reflection on the male math instructors and their delivery of instruction?

Activity #5: A GPA Analysis

As guidance counselor at Horizon High School, you spend considerable time advising high school seniors about attending college. Your local university just announced that it is raising the GPA requirement for admission from 2.8 to 3.0.

Questions

1. Can you produce from the "Horizon High School" data file an analysis of your seniors' GPA in relation to the newly announced GPA requirement at the university?

2. If you analyzed the GPA scores across all grade levels, what concerns might you have?

Discussion

I threw an easier one at you for a change of pace. This issue can be addressed with a simple cross-tabulation, as shown in Table 10.9.

TABLE 10.9 Grade Level by GPA

					GPA				
Grade	2.5	2.8	2.9	3.0	3.1	3.2	3.3	3.4	Total
9th	1	8	3	7	9		5		33
10th	3	4	6	3	8		2		26
11th	7	10		3					20
12th			4	7	5	2	1	2	21
Total	11	22	13	20	22	2	8		100

Things look pretty good with our seniors' GPAs. All but four seniors have GPAs of 3.0 and above, and those four have GPAs very close (2.9). Perhaps we can provide some intervention to assist the four at 2.9. Perhaps they are students planning on attending 2 years at the community college before transferring to the 4-year institution, in which case the issue is not serious.

Wow! The number of students in grades 9, 10, and 11 with noticeably low GPAs is somewhat alarming. Slightly more than 30% of the ninth graders, 50% of tenth graders, and 85% of eleventh graders have GPAs below 3.0. Of special concern is the large group of eleventh graders, for they only have one year to improve significantly. Again, lots of opportunities for instructional data-driven decision making.

Activity 6: One-Way Analysis of Variance (ANOVA)

Having had a close call with the activist parent group over gender equity issues, you, as the Horizon High School principal, decide that you want to look at any significant differences in math scores among the three ethnic groups at your high school. In other words, you are interested to see if any of the three ethnic groups (white, Hispanic, and black) differ significantly from each other in the subject area of math.

A one-way analysis of variance will help address this concern. The ANOVA will reveal any significant differences within any of the comparisons of the three ethnic groups and math scores. In this case, the dependent variable is the math test and the independent (manipulated) variable is the three different ethnic groups. Recall that the ANOVA only indicates whether there is a difference among the three—it does not identify the exact location of the difference. We will need to select a post hoc test (Tukey HSD) to help answer that question.

Recall that the requirement for a t test is that we can compare only two means. This case will have three different means—it is the ANOVA that allows us to compare many means. The mean for the math scores for each of the ethnic groups will be compared with each other: whites with Hispanics, whites with blacks, and Hispanics with blacks. The one-way ANOVA will generate a significance value indicating whether there are significant differences within the comparisons being made. The significance value does not indicate where the difference is or what the differences are, but the post hoc test will help identify pairwise differences.

Questions

1. After running a one-way ANOVA on math scores, run another for each of the other subject areas.

2. With the help of the Tukey HSD test, where does the problem seem to lie?

Discussion

I will not display all of the tables from this analysis. Table 10.10 displays the math analysis, the Tukey test, and an analysis of ethnic groups and writing.

First of all, we realize that the group sizes are unequal in this analysis. In other words, it would be best if all three ethnic groups consisted of similar numbers of students. Admitting a weakness of our study, let's look at the results. The ANOVA reveals a significant difference (or differences) within comparisons of the math scores and the three ethnic groups, based upon a significance level of .026, much lower than our selected .05.

Looking at the Tukey HSD test results, we notice that a significant difference exists between Group 1 (whites) and Group 3 (blacks). The mean difference (5.14) is different enough to be statistically significant at an alpha level just slightly less than our selected .05 (i.e., .045). Though there

TABLE 10.10 One–Way ANOVA and Tukey HSD for Ethnicity and Math Scores

	Descriptives			
	N	*Mean*	*SD*	*Std. Error*
White	56	245.11	7.85	1.05
Hispanic	28	248.43	6.51	1.23
Black	16	250.25	7.72	7.72
Total	100	246.86	7.69	7.69

	ANOVA				
	Sum of Squares	*df*	*Mean Square*	*F*	*Sig.*
Between groups	424.826	2	212.413	3.796	.026
Within groups	5,427.214	97	55.951		
Total	5,852.040	99			

		Tukey HSD Post Hoc Test		
Ethnicity	*Ethnicity*	*Mean Diff.*	*Std. Error*	*Sig.*
White	Hispanic	3.32	1.731	.139
White	Black	5.14*	2.120	.045
Hispanic	Black	1.82	2.344	.718

*Significant at the .05 level.

exists a difference in means between whites and Hispanics (3.32), the difference is not enough to be considered statistically significant. You notice also that the significance level (.139) is much too high to meet the .05 criteria.

Activity 7: Two-Way Analysis of Variance (ANOVA)

Analysis of variance looks for significant differences between groups by comparing the means of those groups with some selected variable. In the one-way analysis of variance described in Activity 6, we were interested to see if the three ethnic groups differed from each other on their performance on standardized math assessment scores. The one-way part of the analysis indicates that there is only one independent variable (three different ethnic groups) and only one dependent variable (math test).

The two-way analysis of variance allows us to use two independent variables. You are interested to discover if there is a relationship (as measured by math scores) between ethnic group and gender (two independent variables). The two-way analysis will allow us to determine if gender or ethnic group or an interaction between gender and ethnic group has an effect on performance in mathematics.

Questions

1. Do females and males differ significantly in math performance as measured by standardized test scores? This question addresses the *main effect* for gender.

2. Do students in the three ethnic groups differ significantly in math performance as measured by standardized test scores? This question addresses the *main effect* for ethnic group.

3. Is there an interaction between gender and ethnic group? This question addresses the possibility, as an example, that Hispanic females score higher in math but white females score lower.

Discussion

Table 10.11 displays descriptive statistics and the ANOVA tests of between-subjects effects.

TABLE 10.11 Two-Way ANOVA for Ethnicity and Math Scores

| Gender/Ethnicity | *Descriptive Statistics* | | |
	Mean	*SD*	*N*
Male			
White	243.73	7.37	37
Hispanic	248.80	7.90	10
Black	249.67	8.26	6
Total	245.36	7.83	53
Female			
White	247.79	8.25	19
Hispanic	248.22	5.85	18
Black	250.60	7.81	10
Total	248.55	7.24	47
Total			
White	245.23	7.85	56
Hispanic	248.43	6.51	28
Black	250.25	7.72	16
Total	246.86	7.69	100

Tests of Between-Subject Effects

Source	Sum of Squares	df	Mean Square	F	Sig.
Gender	38.844	1	38.884	.70	.405
Ethnicity	277.133	2	138.566	2.498	.088
Gender/Ethnicity	99.014	2	49.507	.892	.413

Let's use the information in Table 10.11 to answer the three questions/ hypotheses posed at the beginning of Activity 7:

1. There is no significant main effect for gender. Females (mean = 248.55) did not score significantly higher than males (mean = 245.36), $F = .700, p = .405$.

2. There is no significant main effect for ethnic group. Though the test did not meet the criteria of .05 significance level, .088 is not too distant. We might want to notice a trace of significance between whites and blacks. Blacks had higher scores in both the male and female categories. However, the difference was not great enough to meet our selected .05 criterion.

3. There is no statistically significant interaction between gender and ethnic group.

Conclusion

Argyris and Schoen (1978), in their book, *Organizational Learning,* stated that people function with a gap between their espoused theories (what they believe is the right course of action) and their theories in use (what they choose to do given the surrounding circumstances). Sound like our life in the schools? I think so. They continue by saying that failure to recognize and close those gaps impedes organizational learning.

The data-driven practice field can help close some of those gaps. A crucial component, however, is the opportunity to take what has been learned in the practice field and apply it to the real life of the school and community. So creating practice fields is important but is in itself inadequate (Kim, 1995). There is danger in allowing practice fields to become training grounds as an end in themselves. The learning experiences are no better than our old traditional ways of doing things if they are not moved and adapted to the school workplace.

I continually state that the real culprits in this dilemma are the university teacher and administrator preparation programs. Though there are a few "bright spots" in some preparation programs, for the most part there is no attempt to increase teachers' and administrators' understanding of data analysis or the use of analysis to improve teaching and learning.

Gravetter and Wallnau (2000) introduced their excellent book *Statistics for the Behavioral Sciences* by asking their readers to read the following paragraph, which was adapted from a psychology experiment by Bransford and Johnson (1972). I would like to use the same exercise as a conclusion to this book:

> The procedure is actually quite simple. First you arrange things into different groups depending on their makeup. Of course, one pile may be sufficient, depending on how much there is to do. If you have to go somewhere else due to the lack of facilities, that is the next step; otherwise you are pretty well set. It is important not to overdo any particular endeavor. That is, it is better to do too few things at once than too many. In the short run this may not seem important, but complications from doing too many can easily arise. A mistake can be expensive as well. The manipulations of the appropriate mechanisms should be self-explanatory, and we need not dwell on them here. At first, the whole procedure will seem complicated. Soon, however, it will become just another facet of life. It is difficult to foresee any end to the necessity of this task in the immediate future, but then one never can tell. (p. 4)

Perhaps the above paragraph sounds like some complicated statistical procedure. But it actually describes the everyday task of doing laundry. Knowing this, now go back and read the passage again.

The authors' purpose, like mine here, was to point out the importance of context. When things are out of context, even the simplest procedures can seem complex and difficult to understand. I suggest that this has been one of the problems with the instructional delivery of data-related courses in teacher and administrator preparation programs. They lack context and applicability.

I presented in the preface four important weaknesses of data analysis as presented in most teacher and administrative preparation programs: (a) the irrelevance of statistics to the day-to-day lives of principals and teachers, (b) the lack of integration of current technology into the teaching and learning of statistics, (c) the inappropriate design of statistics courses for teachers and administrators, and (d) the overemphasis on the use of data analysis for research projects and dissertations. I wanted to present a slightly different approach to data analysis in this book. I attempted to emphasize the importance of descriptive analysis and shift the use of inferential analysis from the traditional research and dissertation model to one of relevance and applicability to teachers and administrators.

I firmly believe that until we begin to seriously evaluate and analyze the existing data in our schools, our profession will continue to be scrutinized and questioned with regard to student achievement and quality teaching and learning. There is much evidence indicating that we are losing some of our market share to private schools, vouchers, charter schools, and some emerging for-profit enterprises (Holcomb, 1999). We must discontinue the practice of making decisions based upon intuition and gut feelings.

I sincerely hope that this book, and especially the data-driven practice field, helped to make you more familiar with the data found in your schools. In addition, I hope you see how you can use these existing school data to assist in making sound educational decisions about teaching, learning, and assessment.

Resource A

The t Distribution

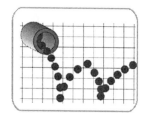

The *t* Distribution

df	Alpha Level					
	0.50	0.20	0.10	0.05	0.02	0.01
1	1.000	3.078	6.314	12.706	31.821	63.657
2	0.816	1.886	2.920	4.303	6.965	9.925
3	0.765	1.638	2.353	3.182	4.541	5.841
4	0.741	1.533	2.132	2.776	3.747	4.604
5	0.727	1.476	2.015	2.571	3.365	4.032
6	0.718	1.440	1.943	2.447	3.143	3.707
7	0.711	1.415	1.895	2.365	2.998	3.499
8	0.706	1.397	1.860	2.306	2.896	3.355
9	0.703	1.383	1.833	2.262	2.821	3.250
10	0.700	1.372	1.812	2.228	2.764	3.169
11	0.697	1.363	1.796	2.201	2.718	3.106
12	0.695	1.356	1.782	2.179	2.681	3.055
13	0.694	1.350	1.771	2.160	2.650	3.012
14	0.692	1.345	1.761	2.145	2.624	2.977
15	0.691	1.341	1.753	2.131	2.602	2.947
16	0.690	1.337	1.746	2.120	2.583	2.921

(continued)

The *t* Distribution *(continued)*

df	Alpha Level					
	0.50	0.20	0.10	0.05	0.02	0.01
17	0.689	1.333	1.740	2.110	2.567	2.898
18	0.688	1.330	1.734	2.101	2.552	2.878
19	0.688	1.328	1.729	2.093	2.539	2.861
20	0.687	1.325	1.725	2.086	2.528	2.845
21	0.686	1.323	1.721	2.080	2.518	2.831
22	0.686	1.321	1.717	2.074	2.508	2.819
23	0.685	1.319	1.714	2.069	2.500	2.807
24	0.685	1.318	1.711	2.064	2.492	2.797
25	0.684	1.316	1.708	2.060	2.485	2.787
26	0.684	1.315	1.706	2.056	2.479	2.779
27	0.684	1.314	1.703	2.052	2.473	2.771
28	0.683	1.313	1.701	2.048	2.467	2.763
29	0.683	1.311	1.699	2.045	2.462	2.756
30	0.683	1.310	1.697	2.042	2.457	2.750
40	0.681	1.303	1.684	2.021	2.423	2.704
50	0.679	1.296	1.671	2.000	2.390	2.660
60	0.677	1.289	1.658	1.980	2.358	2.617
120	0.674	1.282	1.645	1.960	2.326	2.576

Resource B

The F Distribution

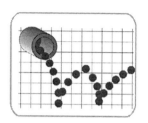

The F Distribution

Table entries are critical values for the 0.05 level of significance.

Denominator: df	Numerator: df									
	1	2	3	4	5	6	7	8	9	10
1	61	200	216	225	230	234	237	239	241	242
2	18.51	19.00	19.16	19.25	19.30	19.33	19.36	19.37	19.38	19.39
3	10.13	9.55	9.28	9.12	9.01	8.94	8.88	8.84	8.81	8.78
4	7.71	6.94	6.59	6.39	6.26	6.16	6.09	6.04	6.00	5.96
5	6.61	5.79	5.41	5.19	5.05	4.95	4.88	4.82	4.78	4.74
6	5.99	5.14	4.76	4.53	4.39	4.28	4.21	4.15	4.10	4.06
7	5.59	4.47	4.35	4.12	3.97	3.87	3.79	3.73	3.68	3.63
8	5.32	4.46	4.07	3.84	3.69	3.58	3.50	3.44	3.39	3.34
9	5.12	4.26	3.86	3.63	3.48	3.37	3.29	3.23	3.18	3.13
10	4.96	4.10	3.71	3.48	3.33	3.22	3.14	3.07	3.02	2.97
11	4.84	3.98	3.59	3.36	3.20	3.09	3.01	2.95	2.90	2.86
12	4.75	3.88	3.49	3.26	3.11	3.00	2.92	2.85	2.80	2.76
13	4.67	3.80	3.41	3.18	3.02	2.92	2.84	2.77	2.72	2.67
14	4.60	3.74	3.34	3.11	2.96	2.85	2.77	2.70	2.65	2.60
15	4.54	3.68	3.29	3.06	2.90	2.79	2.70	2.64	2.59	2.55
16	4.49	3.63	3.24	3.01	2.85	2.74	2.66	2.59	2.54	2.49
17	4.45	3.59	3.20	2.96	2.81	2.70	2.62	2.55	2.50	2.45

df										
18	4.41	3.55	3.16	2.93	2.77	2.66	2.58	2.51	2.46	2.41
19	4.38	3.52	3.13	2.90	2.74	2.63	2.55	2.48	2.43	2.38
20	4.35	3.49	3.10	2.87	2.71	2.60	2.52	2.45	2.40	2.35
21	4.32	3.47	3.07	2.84	2.68	2.57	2.49	2.42	2.37	2.32
22	4.30	3.44	3.05	2.82	2.66	2.55	2.47	2.40	2.35	2.30
23	4.28	3.42	3.03	2.80	2.64	2.53	2.45	2.38	2.32	2.28
24	4.26	3.40	3.01	2.78	2.62	2.51	2.43	2.36	2.30	2.26
25	4.24	3.38	2.99	2.76	2.60	2.49	2.41	2.34	2.28	2.24
26	4.22	3.37	2.98	2.74	2.59	2.47	2.39	2.32	2.27	2.22
27	4.21	3.35	2.96	2.73	2.57	2.46	2.37	2.30	2.25	2.20
28	4.20	3.34	2.95	2.71	2.56	2.44	2.36	2.29	2.24	2.19
29	4.18	3.33	2.93	2.70	2.54	2.43	2.35	2.28	2.22	2.18
30	4.17	3.32	2.92	2.69	2.53	2.42	2.34	2.27	2.21	2.16
32	4.15	3.30	2.90	2.67	2.51	2.40	2.32	2.25	2.19	2.14
34	4.13	3.28	2.88	2.65	2.49	2.38	2.30	2.23	2.17	2.12
36	4.11	3.26	2.86	2.63	1.48	2.36	2.28	2.21	2.15	2.10
38	4.10	3.25	2.85	2.62	2.46	2.35	2.26	2.19	2.14	2.09
40	4.08	3.23	2.84	2.61	2.45	2.34	2.25	2.18	2.12	2.07
42	4.07	3.22	2.83	2.59	2.44	2.32	2.24	2.17	2.11	2.06
44	4.06	3.21	2.82	2.58	2.43	3.31	2.23	2.16	2.10	2.05
46	4.05	3.20	2.81	2.57	2.42	2.30	2.22	2.14	2.09	2.04
48	4.04	3.19	2.80	2.56	2.41	2.30	2.21	2.14	2.08	2.03
50	4.03	3.18	2.79	2.56	2.40	2.29	2.20	2.13	2.07	2.02

Resource C

Music Correlation

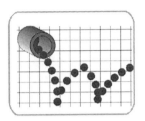

Music Correlation

Students	Band	Math	Language	Science
1	3	220	215	220
2	4	240	210	225
3	2.5	210	250	235
4	2	215	230	210
5	4	260	240	220
6	3	230	270	250
7	3.5	240	240	220
8	4	259	220	240
9	3	245	230	250
10	4	280	270	230
11	4.5	300	260	220
12	2	230	250	225
13	3	250	245	235
14	4	275	235	210
15	2.5	200	260	220
16	2	200	255	250
17	4	290	250	220
18	3	250	230	240
19	3.5	270	245	250
20	4	280	270	230
21	3	260	270	260
22	4	270	250	230
23	4.5	310	260	280
24	2	170	250	220

Resource D

Horizon High School Data

Horizon High School Data

Students	Gender	Ethnic	Freeredu	Math	Language	Science	Writing	Grade	GPA
1	1	1	1	234	248	239	175	9	2.8
2	2	2	2	239	242	242	188	11	2.5
3	1	2	1	263	258	263	200	12	3
4	2	1	1	244	244	239	212	10	2.8
5	1	2	1	247	243	245	196	9	2.8
6	2	1	1	257	259	247	198	9	3
7	1	1	2	239	252	244	211	11	2.8
8	1	2	2	248	252	243	187	12	3.2
9	2	1	2	247	249	253	221	12	3.1
10	1	1	2	234	245	239	190	10	3.1
11	2	3	2	247	248	247	222	11	2.8
12	1	3	2	247	254	242	214	10	2.5
13	1	1	2	239	240	245	197	10	3
14	1	3	1	247	247	236	190	9	3.1
15	2	1	2	247	232	244	189	9	3.3
16	2	3	2	263	240	239	187	9	3
17	1	2	2	244	242	242	211	11	2.8
18	2	3	1	247	250	263	214	12	3
19	1	2	2	257	248	276	221	10	2.9
20	1	1	2	239	250	245	189	9	3.1

21	1	1	2	248	259	247	190	9	2.8
22	2	2	1	247	252	244	214	11	2.5
23	1	1	2	234	252	266	234	12	3.2
24	2	2	2	247	249	253	212	12	3.1
25	2	2	2	247	240	239	189	10	2.8
26	2	1	1	239	248	247	198	11	3
27	2	2	2	247	254	242	211	10	2.8
28	1	1	1	247	240	267	214	10	2.9
29	2	1	1	234	247	236	189	9	2.9
30	1	3	1	239	249	244	190	9	3.1
31	2	3	1	263	240	239	189	9	2.8
32	1	1	2	244	242	242	214	11	2.5
33	1	2	2	247	258	263	199	12	3
34	2	2	2	257	244	239	212	10	3.1
35	1	1	2	239	243	245	197	9	2.5
36	2	3	2	248	259	247	198	9	3
37	1	1	2	247	252	244	211	11	2.8
38	1	1	2	234	252	239	214	12	3.4
39	1	1	1	247	249	253	221	12	3.1
40	2	2	2	247	256	239	231	10	3.1
41	2	1	2	239	248	247	222	11	2.8

(continued)

Horizon High School Data (continued)

Students	Gender	Ethnic	Freeredu	Math	Language	Science	Writing	Grade	GPA
42	1	2	2	247	254	242	214	10	2.5
43	2	1	1	255	240	256	213	10	3
44	1	3	2	263	247	236	189	9	3.1
45	1	1	2	244	256	244	200	9	3.3
46	1	1	2	247	240	239	196	9	3
47	2	2	1	257	242	242	211	11	2.8
48	1	1	2	239	258	263	214	12	2.9
49	2	2	2	248	244	239	221	10	2.9
50	2	2	2	247	243	245	201	9	3.1
51	2	2	1	234	259	247	203	9	2.8
52	2	1	2	239	252	244	214	11	2.5
53	1	1	1	263	252	220	217	12	3
54	2	1	1	244	249	253	212	12	3.1
55	1	1	1	254	256	239	216	10	3.3
56	2	3	1	257	248	247	198	11	3
57	1	2	2	239	254	242	211	10	3.1
58	1	1	2	248	240	240	214	10	2.9
59	2	1	2	247	247	236	189	9	2.9
60	1	1	2	234	240	244	187	9	3.1

61	2	3	2	247	240	239	200	9	2.8
62	1	1	2	247	242	242	214	11	2.5
63	1	2	2	239	258	263	211	12	3
64	1	1	1	253	244	239	212	10	3.1
65	2	3	2	247	243	245	199	9	3.3
66	2	1	2	263	259	247	198	9	3
67	1	1	2	244	252	244	211	11	2.8
68	2	2	1	255	252	254	214	12	2.9
69	1	2	2	257	260	253	221	12	2.9
70	1	1	2	239	245	239	231	10	3.1
71	1	1	2	248	248	247	222	11	2.8
72	2	2	1	250	254	242	214	10	2.5
73	1	1	2	234	240	245	197	10	3
74	2	2	2	247	247	236	190	9	3.1
75	2	2	2	247	245	244	200	9	3.3
76	2	1	1	239	240	239	198	9	3
77	2	1	2	247	242	242	211	11	2.8
78	1	1	1	250	258	263	214	12	3.4
79	2	1	1	250	244	239	221	10	2.9
80	1	1	1	245	243	245	186	9	3.1
81	2	1	1	263	259	247	199	9	2.8

(continued)

Horizon High School Data (continued)

Students	Gender	Ethnic	Freeredu	Math	Language	Science	Writing	Grade	GPA
82	1	1	2	244	252	244	214	11	2.5
83	1	1	2	247	252	240	213	12	3
84	2	1	2	257	249	253	212	12	3.1
85	1	1	2	239	250	239	200	10	3.3
86	2	3	2	248	248	247	198	11	3
87	1	1	2	247	254	242	211	10	2.8
88	1	1	2	234	240	238	214	10	2.9
89	1	3	1	255	247	236	200	9	2.9
90	2	1	2	247	245	244	199	9	3.1
91	2	3	2	239	240	239	201	9	2.8
92	1	3	2	247	242	242	214	11	2.5
93	2	1	1	250	258	263	198	12	3
94	1	1	2	263	244	239	212	10	3.1
95	1	1	2	244	243	245	200	9	3.3
96	1	1	2	247	259	247	198	9	3
97	2	2	1	257	252	244	211	11	2.8
98	1	1	2	239	252	260	214	12	3.3
99	2	2	2	248	249	253	221	12	2.9
100	2	2	2	247	238	239	202	10	3.1

References

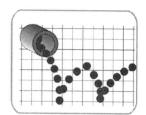

Argyris, C., & Schoen, D. (1978). *Organizational learning: A theory of action perspective.* Reading, MA: Addison-Wesley.

Bracey, G. (1997). *Understanding education statistics: It's easier (and more important) than you think.* Arlington, VA: Educational Research Service.

Bransford, J., & Johnson, M. (1972). Contextual prerequisites for understanding: Some investigations of comprehension and recall. *Journal of Verbal Learning and Verbal Behavior, 11,* 717-772.

Creighton, T. (1999). Standards: The Idaho horizon. *Perspectives [Idaho Association of School Administrators], 16*(4), 8-13.

Fitch, M., & Malcom, P. (1998). Using data effectively for school improvement planning. *Effective School Report for Research and Practice, 16*(6), 1, 4-5.

Gravetter, F., & Wallnau, L. (2000). *Statistics for the behavioral sciences.* Belmount, CA: Wadsworth.

Griffiths, D. (1998). *Educational administration: Reform PDQ or RIP* (Occasional Paper No. 8312). Tempe, AZ: University Council for Educational Administration.

Holcomb, E. (1999). *Getting excited about data: How to combine people, passion, and proof.* Thousand Oaks, CA: Corwin.

Kim, D. (1995). Managerial practice fields. In S. Chawla & J. Renesch (Eds.), *Learning organizations: Developing cultures for tomorrow's workplace.* Portland: Productivity Press.

McNamara, J. (1996). *Teaching statistics in principal preparation programs.* College Station: Texas A & M University, Research Department.

Milstein, M. (1990). Rethinking the clinical aspects of preparation programs: From theory to practice. In S. L. Jacobson & J. A. Conway (Eds.), *Educational leadership in an age of reform (pp. 119-130). New York: Longman.*

MPR Associates Inc. (1998). *At your fingertips: Using everyday data to improve schools.* Brisbane, CA: George Lithograph.

Murphy, J., & Forsyth, P. (1999). A decade of change: An overview. In J. Murphy & P. Forsyth (Eds.), *Educational administration: A decade of reform* (pp. 3-38). Thousand Oaks, CA: Corwin.

Runyan, R., Haber, A., & Coleman, K. (1994). *Behavioral statistics: The core.* New York: McGraw-Hill.

Senge, P. (1990). *The fifth discipline: The art and practice of the learning organization.* New York: Doubleday.

Index

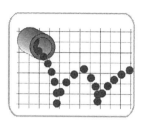

CORWIN
PRESS

The Corwin Press logo—a raven striding across an open book—represents the happy union of courage and learning. We are a professional-level publisher of books and journals for K–12 educators, and we are committed to creating and providing resources that embody these qualities. Corwin's motto is "Success for All Learners."